D0204092

Communication and *Turnip's Blood*
by Rachel Maddux

Communication,

the Autobiography

of Rachel Maddux,

and Her Novella,

Turnip's Blood

Edited, with an introduction,
by Nancy A. Walker

The University of Tennessee Press
KNOXVILLE

Library of Congress Cataloging in Publication Data

Maddux, Rachel, 1913—1983.
     [Communication]
     Communication, the autobiography of Rachel Maddux, and her novella,
Turnip's blood / edited, with an introduction, by Nancy A. Walker.—1st ed.
          p. cm.
     ISBN 0-87049-699-9 (cloth : alk. pa.)
     1. Maddux, Rachel, 1913–1983 — Biography 2. Novelists,
American—20th century—Biography. I. Walker, Nancy A., 1942–   .
II. Maddux, Rachel, 1913–1983. Turnip's blood. c1991. III. Title.
PS3563.A3395Z464   1991
813' . 54—dc20
[B]   91-7248
                 CIP

To Savington Crampton

Contents

Turnip's Blood
by Rachel Maddux   159

A Bibliography of the Published
Works of Rachel Maddux   211

Illustrations

Preface

The discovery of this manuscript and the process of bringing it to publication have become part of our own autobiographies.

We wish to thank those who have helped to make this project possible. Savington Crampton, who safeguarded the manuscript of *Communication* for fifty years before its publication, was generous in his sharing of letters and memories. Savington and Honor Crampton provided gracious hospitality to both of us at different times in their home near Sarasota, Florida. Carol Wallace Orr, Director of the University of Tennessee Press, immediately recognized the value of this manuscript. We also wish to thank Katherine B. Brown; Melissa Baker Edwards; Howard Gotlieb and the staff in Special Collections at the Boston University Mugar Memorial Library; Thomas D. Lane; W. Sidney Vinson III; and Carrie Chappell Wiltshire. Special thanks are due to Russell G. Hamilton, Dean of Graduate Studies and Research at Vanderbilt University, who provided research funding for the project.

Maddux's own notes to the text of *Communication* appear at the foot of each page. The editor's notes appear following the text of the autobiography.

It has been a joy for the two of us to work together to bring to readers Rachel Maddux's autobiography and its companion piece, her first published story, *Turnip's Blood.*

NANCY A. WALKER
SUSAN FORD WILTSHIRE

Nashville, Tennessee
November 19, 1990

Foreword

Rachel Maddux wrote her autobiography at the age of twenty-eight. The fact that *Communication* is being published posthumously, fifty years after it was written, would not surprise its remarkable author. She would simply nod and smile.

I first heard of Rachel Maddux from friends who spoke of a writer in rural Tennessee who sometimes attended the Friends Meeting in Nashville. Several years later I read her novel *A Walk in the Spring Rain* and saw in the credits Rachel's expression of gratitude to the agricultural agent of the same county where my family has a farm sixty miles west of Nashville. As soon as I realized that Rachel lived nearby, I drove over one Sunday afternoon in 1976 to meet her.

She and her husband, King Baker, were away, but a young man tending the orchard in their absence invited me into the house to leave a note. The first thing I noticed was an inscribed photograph of a radiant Ingrid Bergman, with her arms around Rachel's goats, taken while Bergman and Anthony Quinn were filming *A Walk in the Spring Rain*. (Later, when I helped prepare Rachel's papers for the Special Collections Library at Boston University, I found a file of affectionate letters sent by Bergman to Rachel from all over the world.)

I returned the next week. Rachel welcomed me warmly and offered a glass of cool well water. With her no-waste economy of gesture, she invited me to sit down at her dining table where we immediately began talking about creativity in children. Rachel was certain that children are born with creativity and educated out of it. Otherwise, she asked, why are most children creative at the age of two and most not by the age of fifteen? To be creative, she insisted, you must be your own child.

My friendship with Rachel began that day and lasted until her death seven years later. Once or twice a month, I would drive to the orchard on Sunday afternoons for a good talk, often jotting down our conversations in a small notebook in my lap. Sometimes I took my friends to meet Rachel. Frequently I met friends of hers who also had come to visit.

One of her friends, perhaps the closest of all, I came to know through his phone calls to the orchard every Sunday afternoon at 3:00. Savington Crampton met Rachel in 1937 when, en route from New York to his job in Hollywood as a radio producer, he stopped in Kansas City to meet the author after reading *Turnip's Blood*. A brilliant intellectual who still reads Latin for pleasure and exercises the same acute critical judgment that brought him to Rachel's door in the first place, Savvy always supported Rachel and her work. For example, when she wrote about a new part-time job, "Here I am with another crummy job, Savvy," he responded, "You cannot afford a good job. It would cost too much."

Savvy was not Rachel's mentor, because she created herself. But, as she relates in *Communication*, he confirmed her vocation as a writer; he became one of the models for Justin Magnus in *The Green Kingdom*; and he stood by her as a friend and intellectual companion for forty-six years. "We were always a little ahead of each other," he recalls. "Nothing ever needed any footnotes." In a journal entry of 1946, Rachel noted: "I never feel really out of touch with Savvy. God love him. There is no one quite like him. There is no one who makes me feel quite so valuable—such an asset to the world." Rachel and Savvy were flint for each other's steel.

Savvy was pleased that a classics professor was among Rachel's friends in Tennessee, and sometimes he and I would talk during the Sunday conversations about a quotation from Catullus or a passage from Vergil. I was delighted when he sent me his new *Oxford Latin Dictionary* as a gift, explaining that as he neared ninety he had decided his smaller one would suffice.

A year after Rachel died, I visited Savvy and his wife, Honor Crampton, at their home in Florida. With the same quick empathy I had experienced with Rachel, we discussed many subjects of common interest in addition to those touching on our mutual friend. As I left, Savvy handed me a slender manuscript Rachel had given him shortly after it was written. It was a typed carbon on onionskin paper, slightly over a hundred pages in length, divided by different colors of construction paper that had been cut and stapled to create chapters in the text. The manuscript was the sole copy of *Communication*, and it is to Savington Crampton that we owe its survival.

Although I thought I knew Rachel well, I was daunted by this startlingly bold account of a childhood and young adulthood different from anything or anyone I had ever known. Perhaps also because I was still grieving Rachel's death, I put the manuscript aside for several years.

Then, in the same summer that I wrote brief memoirs of Rachel and other significant women in my life, I began to realize the value of this manuscript in which a writer resolutely refuses to romanticize her youth or deny the pain and anger it contained. Savvy and I agreed that it was time to send *Communication* to a publisher. Because the University of Tennessee Press had published *Fiction into Film*, an account of the turning of *A Walk in the Spring Rain* into a movie, I sent the manuscript to director Carol Orr. A week later, Ms. Orr called to say she wanted to publish *Communication*. "Why?" I asked. "Because I believe every word Rachel Maddux wrote." "Why do you want your press to publish it?" I persisted. "Because she was writing fifty years ahead of her time."

One crucial role remained to be cast. Without knowing it, we were all waiting for Nancy Walker.

It is very difficult for people who knew Rachel personally to write about her. She was at the same time powerful and tender, with so many intellectual and emotional facets that to present her whole is a defeating prospect. Katherine Brown, her close friend from Kansas City and later neighbor at the orchard, tried to write about Rachel and gave up. I pieced together a personal memoir but knew I could never undertake a full accounting.

Nancy Walker had just come to Vanderbilt as a professor of English and director of the women's studies program when I asked her to take a look at the manuscript. Her letter to Carol Orr outlining its importance was so compelling that she was invited to write the introduction. With her background in women's fiction and autobiography, Walker combines the intellectual skills and clarity of mind required to place *Communication* and Rachel's work in context. Although Walker has come to identify closely with her subject, sometimes with uncanny percipience, she has never lost the perspective necessary for critical analysis.

Rachel Maddux's impact on the people who knew her was closely connected with the power of her writing. Martin Quigley, in his memoir about Kansas City journalism in the thirties, recalls the gatherings of young writers at Rachel's apartment at 16 West 43rd, which he called "the only Bohemia in town." Rachel urged the group gathered around her to produce a literary journal. The journal never appeared, but it was in that apartment that Rachel wrote *Turnip's Blood*, the work that established her as a writer.

Rachel did not so much bring out the best in people as bring out something they did not know was there. Once she succeeded in persuading me to play a Haydn duet with her on her small spinet. This came as quite a surprise to me since I hardly play the piano.

Rachel's writing rose out of her courage and her unreasonable love for the world. She summarized her religion in three words: "Everyone is me." Her definition of human rights was equally terse: "It's a pretty hard passage down the birth canal, and anyone who makes it has a right to be here."

Her conscience fueled her writing. In *Communication* she tells about becoming ill as a child because she could not prevent an execution at the state prison. Later she wrote a letter to the governor seeking pardon for a man who was about to receive a long term for stealing chickens to feed his motherless children.

The governor pardoned the man as a result of Rachel's letter and wrote to tell her so. She says that she was very impressed by what could be accomplished by the written word of a child. "This writing, I thought, is a serious thing, not to be fooled around with. Perhaps that is where my respect for the written word comes from."

Rachel's sensitivity is poignantly reflected in her novel *Abel's Daughter*, which tells of a friendship between two young women, one white, one black, in Virginia during World War II. The friend who inspired the novel corresponded with Rachel for years afterward, sometimes sending photographs of her daughter whom she had named Rachel. Rachel's adopted daughter Melissa also named her daughter, born after Rachel's death, for her mother.

Rachel wrote out of her adamant refusal ever to deny her loneliness or to divide private life from public. "To write," she said to me once, "you have to be willing to lie naked on the dining room table in the middle of the interstate." She was quite clear-headed about the creative process. "Write with your creative self," she urged. "Then go over it again with your corrective self." Once she admonished me perceptively, "Creativity is not subject to control. And I imagine it's hard for you to give up control."

She warned never to make excuses for not writing and in particular to avoid the "cabin in the woods" syndrome, as in "I could write if only I had a cabin in the woods." "The demands of one's own work," she remarked on one occasion, "unlike those sometimes imposed by other people, never seem outrageous. 'Yassuh,' we say obsequiously, 'Yassuh.' Shuffle, shuffle."

On another Sunday afternoon visit, she observed: "The difficult thing isn't writing. That's easy. The difficult thing is waiting to write." The waiting is especially evident in her only nonfiction work, *The Orchard Children*. Rachel told me it took thirteen years of waiting before she could write that book because "it took that long to leave enough out."

Creativity is measured by one's response not to success but to failure. Among Rachel's papers was a large poster board, carefully marked into a grid. In the left-hand column were the names of five or six short stories she had submitted for publication. There was one column for the date mailed, another for the cost of the postage, still another for the date of receipt the manuscript was acknowledged. The final column was headed "Accepted or rejected." All the stories had been rejected.

Once I was with Rachel when she opened a letter from her agent who had been trying unsuccessfully to place one of her stories. The letter consisted of four words: "I don't give up."

"Ah," smiled Rachel, "those wonderful four-word letters."

A careless observer could confuse Rachel's tenderness with pessimism. She said once to me, "Life after all is fair; ultimately it breaks everybody's heart." Rachel's writing and life, however, were braced with remarkable resilience and laced with humor. After King's death, the orchard froze for two successive years and she was in desperate financial straits. She never gave up. "I'm going to write my way out of this," she said through clenched teeth. Her humor was inwrought with her wry view of the human condition. "When I am dictator, . . ." she liked to intone with a grin whenever she heard of some egregious injustice. Once when an interviewer asked her if she believed in heaven, she demurred. He pressed her: "Well, if you did, whom would you want to see there?" Instantly she replied, "You mean after former lovers?"

Rachel taught those around her by her tenderness and love, her relentless care for the written and spoken word, and her lifetime play of showdown hands. Pain was her teacher, and she was patient enough to wait for the truth and the words. But she also believed we are meant to be happy. I cannot say whether at the end she was happy. She was, however, grappling rather than buffeted—the condition she identifies in the preface to *The Green Kingdom* as constituting the climate of potentiality.

In her last illness, Rachel asked me to find a recording of the musical *Carnival*, in which the character Lilly sings of coming from a town called Mira "where everybody knew my name." I played a cassette of the recording for Rachel as she was drifting in and out of consciousness, every breath a contest with the cancer that was consuming her. Remembering that she had told me once that hearing was the last sense to leave a dying person, I said to her:

"Rachel, you have written beautiful books, you have touched a thousand lives, and a lot of people know your name."

She smiled, her eyes closed, and said, "Yes, it's nice, isn't it?"

She died two days later on November 19, 1983, at the age of seventy.

SUSAN FORD WILTSHIRE
Vanderbilt University

Introduction

1. *Communication*

"It is my privilege to do myself justice." With these words Rachel Maddux begins her autobiography, and so sums up the act of autobiography itself: the opportunity to present to the reader a self of one's own choosing, selecting from among many facts, memories, and experiences those that will compose the public self. "Of course I shall be prejudiced," Maddux also writes. Of course. Yet it is uncommon for the author of an autobiography to so candidly announce his or her selectivity and control of the text. Maddux even tells the reader the sorts of things she feels free to omit from her account: for example, her adolescent infatuation with a Swedish cello player, and the time she "hit Eloise Haycraft over the head with a doll buggy." The cello player is, indeed, nowhere to be found in the pages that follow, but the incident with Eloise and the doll buggy finds its way after all into the account, as if to underscore Maddux's power to control her own story.

Such power—and the candor with which it is expressed—is only one of several elements that make Rachel Maddux's *Communication: Being the Mental Autobiography of a Sturdy Quest* an unusual and compelling autobiography. Perhaps the most important of these is the date of its composition and the age of its author. When Rachel Maddux died in November of 1983, she was nearly seventy-one; yet *Communication* was written in 1941, when she was twenty-eight. At the time she completed *Communication*, Maddux had just begun her career as a published writer; she had published the novella *Turnip's Blood* in *Story* magazine in

December of 1936, and had encountered great good luck for a beginning writer: *Turnip's Blood*, with four other novellas, was reprinted in a collection titled *The Flying Yorkshireman* that was a Book-of-the-Month Club selection in May of 1938. Two more of Maddux's stories were published in *Story* in 1938, fulfilling the prophecy of the 1936 contributor's note, which described Maddux as "a new author whom we shall probably hear more of later."[1] She was, then, at the start of a promising career, not at its culminating point—her name was not then, and is not now, a household word.

Rather than the summing up of a life, Maddux's autobiography is precisely what its title suggests: the record of a search for true communication with another person that had occupied Maddux's youth and that had not ceased at the time of its composition. Addressed to a specific individual, *Communication* was not published during her lifetime, nor was that Maddux's intent.[2] But the intensity of her desire to be understood—and in the process to better understand herself—suggests that fifty years later she would not object to speaking to readers more ready to understand her now than they would have been in 1941.

During her lifetime, Rachel Maddux published three novels, one work of non-fiction, and a half-dozen stories. Although she was not a prolific author, she worked steadily, sure of her vocation, while battling poor health, the rootlessness of the war years, disillusionment with the urbanization of southern California, and finally the isolation of rural Tennessee, where she lived for the last twenty-three years of her life. Maddux's published work has received little critical attention, but it constitutes a vivid reflection of significant social and cultural issues during the mid-twentieth century: the search for a re-ordering of human priorities during a time of depression and war in *The Green Kingdom*, race relations in *Abel's Daughter*, a woman finding love in middle age in *A Walk in the Spring Rain*, and the plight of abandoned children in *The Orchard Children*. Maddux's fiction—especially *Abel's Daughter*—has strong autobiographical elements, revealing the unflinching devotion to human dignity and individual singularity that also characterizes *Communication.*

Written before Rachel Maddux wrote her major fiction and non-fiction works, *Communication* was not a gesture to a reading public to whom she had an established significance, but rather an attempt to explain herself to someone she thought capable of understanding her.

Carolyn Heilbrun, in *Writing a Woman's Life*, identifies four ways in which a woman's life may be written:

> The woman herself may tell it, in what she chooses to call an autobiography; she may tell it in what she chooses to call fiction; a biographer, woman or man, may write the woman's life in what is called biography; or the woman may write her own life in advance of living it, unconsciously, and without recognizing or naming the process.[3]

The existence of Rachel Maddux's *Communication* blurs the edges of Heilbrun's categories. Maddux does "name the process"; that is, she consciously wrote an autobiography. But the fact that she did so in advance of the remaining forty-two years of her life suggests that she was in part establishing a framework for those remaining years. By daring to say at twenty-eight, "this is who I am," Maddux sets forth themes and motifs that would later appear in her published work—the love of music, children, and animals; a constant search for *essences.* She also details the formation of convictions and characteristics that would inform her choices and behavior for the rest of her life: a fierce honesty, a belief in the dignity of all humanity, and a rigorous self-scrutiny.

It is these qualities, so clearly in evidence in *Communication,* that Heilbrun finds missing in many other autobiographies by women. Accustomed to practicing an automatic, unconscious self-censorship—especially with regard to such emotions as anger—women have followed what Heilbrun terms "the old genre of female autobiography, which tends to find beauty even in pain and to transform rage into spiritual acceptance" (12). "Above all other prohibitions," Heilbrun writes, "what has been forbidden to women is anger, together with the open admission of the desire for power and control over one's life (which necessarily means accepting some degree of power and control over other lives)" (13). She points to the example of May Sarton's *Plant Dreaming Deep*, in which Sarton suppresses the pain and anger of her isolation, emotions that Sarton later expressed in *Journal of a Solitude*. Of more direct relevance to Maddux's *Communication* is Eudora Welty's *One Writer's Beginnings*, which also explores a writer's early years, but does so with a nostalgia for childhood that Heilbrun finds false and even dangerous in its suppression of feelings considered "unfeminine."

No such nostalgia attends *Communication*. The childhood that Maddux evokes has its share of pain, anger, and isolation, none of it veiled or ameliorated by wistful sentimentality. Eloise Haycraft invited a blow to the head with the doll buggy by threatening the well-being of Maddux's teddy bear, and remains unforgiven: "I never changed my feeling toward her. I suppose I hate her yet."[4] Of greater significance is Maddux's account of trying to please her stern and distant father, whose periodic rages terrorized the household. "Children," she writes, "do not like comfort. They worship whoever demands the most of them. Therefore, I sought his attention." Although by the age of twenty-eight Maddux understands that fear and boredom were the sources of her father's behavior, she neither excuses him nor downplays her own fear and sense of rejection.

Not all of the pain recorded in *Communication* is emotional. Some of the most vivid sequences in the autobiography describe Maddux's coming to understand and deal with physical illness. She alludes to illness in early infancy ("I very nearly died at first") and tells of having smallpox at the age of three, but what shadows her youth is a series of headaches and blackouts that were only much later diagnosed as *petit mal* epilepsy.[5] Caught between a hypochondriac father and a mother who had "the country woman's distrust of medicines and fear of drugs," Maddux, at the age of ten, decided that there was a connection between the headaches and her fears, and set about to conquer those fears—

fears of trains, of walking on sand or gravel, of her father's loud swearing. When finally her epilepsy is diagnosed, the neurologist points out the single connection that the ten-year-old Maddux did not make: her fears were all related to sounds—noises capable of triggering neurological imbalance.

But *Communication* is far from being wholly a record of suffering, though the manner in which its author describes and deals with painful experiences is one element that sets it apart from most other examples of the autobiographical genre. Maddux tells of many joys and triumphs in her first twenty-eight years, some that link her with the life patterns of many other women who have written their lives, and others that speak to sensibilities that her later writing, both fiction and nonfiction, would identify as uniquely her own. Maddux's relationship with her sister, Erma, reminds us in its intensity of the relationships between women so frequently described in women's autobiographical writing. In one sense, Maddux feels that she owes Erma her life (and in a way repaid that debt by naming after her the central female character in her 1957 novel *The Green Kingdom*): after her parents' decision that two children (Erma and Victor) were "sufficient," Erma's fervent desire for a sister helped to change their minds. Rachel was their third child. One of the threads in *Communication* is Maddux's movement away from the values and habits of thought of her parents and toward Erma, with whom she first approximates the kind of "communication" she seeks so fervently. Maddux's detachment from each of her parents and her recognition of Erma's special qualities occur as precise, crystalline moments. Instructed by her father never to admit to ignorance in school, Maddux recalls a day in grade school when she suddenly thought, "My father is wrong about this," and confesses to not knowing an answer rather than bluffing. "That day," she writes, "I was free of his mind." Her rejection of her mother's values occurs later, at the point when she has taken command of her own health and has consulted a doctor about her back pain and her blackouts. When her mother expresses dismay that Maddux has confessed to the latter—"He will think you have *fits*"—Maddux suddenly sees her mother's reaction as part of a pattern of behavior, "the long, long line of little subterfuges and hypocrisies and glossings of the truth," and, as she had done with her father, she rejects this parental model: "I did not understand her yet and I hated her methods and I knew once and for always that they could never be mine." While the word "yet" in this statement points toward Maddux's eventual reconciliation with her mother, her decision to avoid subterfuge was total and life-long.

It is this commitment to honesty that makes Maddux's relationship with Erma so special. Eight years older than Maddux, Erma had long been the adored but remote older sister—"I had held onto her as the one perfect being I had ever known"—but when they come together as young adults, Maddux for the first time finds someone who actually listens to her and respects the way her mind works—respects, in short, her singularity as a human being:

> [Erma] had, among hundreds, two very rare qualities. One was that she took it for granted that you were responsible, were, in fact, an authority for your own statements. To your statements she only applied your interpretations. Her own interpretations she applied to her own statements. The other quality was that each day died at sunset. She never reminded you today of what you had said yesterday.

Erma's gift to Rachel is thus her own authority, the right to her own autonomy and expertise, and by extension, the right to be the *author* of her own life. Erma also provides remarkably feminist support—in what must have been about 1930—for Maddux's ambition to be a doctor: "She did NOT remind me that I was a girl. She did NOT remind me of my health. She did not tell me that as soon as I got married I would get over all that." (Maddux did later begin medical school, but poor health forced her to drop out.)[6] Fittingly, Erma was also responsible for Maddux's first publication; she read the manuscript of *Turnip's Blood* and sent it to *Story* magazine, where it was published in 1936.

Toward the end of her life, Maddux recalled an incident that crystallized both her adoration of her older sister and the problematic relationship with her father. In a letter to Savington Crampton dated July 31, 1981, and written during a period of severe financial difficulty and failing health, Maddux reports her struggles to remain, unlike her father, an optimist:

> The Fates have been trying to make a pessimist out of me for a long time and By God they just may succeed. My father would be so satisfied if I had finally made it to join the depressed people like himself "who had sense enough to worry." One of our earliest conversations (I am wearing my new burgundy winter coat just finished by my mother. Made from Erma's coat):
>
> Father: How can you look so goddamned cheerful in a second-hand coat?
>
> Me (stroking lapels): Why Papa, it's easy. It was Erma's.

The period of late adolescence in Rachel Maddux's life is crowned with triumphs of the mind, confirmation of her intellectual abilities. In a comparative anatomy course, she becomes the first person to dissect out the last cranial nerve of the shark, and reports, "I have rarely been so happy." In a class on Greek sculpture, she sets the frieze on the Parthenon to music by assigning note values to the vertical and horizontal distances between parts of the figures. The beginning of her successful career as an author with the publication of *Turnip's Blood*, which occupies the penultimate chapter of *Communication*, is the logical outgrowth of the intellectual development that is Maddux's central concern in her autobiography.

During the past twenty years, the study of women's autobiographical writing has become increasingly complex and sophisticated, revising definitions of autobiographical genre and individual selfhood that had been predicated on male-authored autobiographies beginning in the 1950s. Recognizing that the very concepts of "self" and "individuality" are socially constructed, feminist scholars have pointed to the radically different relationship that women have had to these concepts. Whereas traditional approaches to autobiography have emphasized the rational, detached recording of experiences and achievements that reflect one's progress through a particular historical moment, we have come to recognize that cultural marginalizing and various forms of silencing have deeply problematized women's relationship to self-representation. Not only are the forms in which women write of themselves often different—e.g., letters, diaries, and journals—but even within the formal memior or autobiography women display an awareness of being subject and object simultaneously: formulating a self that has in turn been formulated by the social constructions of gender.

Bella Brodzki and Celeste Schenck articulate this point within the context of contemporary theories of male and female relation to selfhood:

> No mirror of *her* era, the female autobiographer takes as a given that selfhood is mediated; her invisibility results from her lack of a tradition, her marginality in male-dominated culture, her fragmentation—social and political as well as psychic. At both extremes of subjectivity and publicity, the female autobiographer has lacked the sense of radical individuality, duplicitous but useful, that empowered Augustine and Henry Adams to write their representative lives large.[7]

Unusual as it is in other ways, Maddux's *Communication* also presents a singular instance. At the age of twenty-eight, Rachel Maddux makes no claim to be representative; indeed, she is instead concerned with uniqueness—with "rachelness"—which has both joyous potential and an isolating loneliness. Convinced that she possesses an essential and inviolable "self," Maddux's search for "communication" is a search for someone who will respect that essence rather than imposing upon it his or her own expectations and requirements.

Such a search, paradoxically, involves Maddux in the relational quest for an "other," similar to the presence that Mary G. Mason describes in her essay "The Other Voice." Mason argues that the patterns for autobiography established by Augustine's and Rousseau's *Confessions*—patterns involving the triumph of the individual—are not echoed in women's autobiographical writing:

> The self-discovery of female identity seems to acknowledge the real presence and recognition of another consciousness, and the disclosure of female self is linked to the identification of some "other." This recognition of another consciousness ... this grounding of identity through relation to the chosen other, seems ... to enable women to write openly about themselves.[8]

The "other" in relation to which women find identity may, especially in earlier centuries, be a divine being who serves as "Creator, Father, and Lover" (210), or it may be an earthly father or husband. Thus Anne Bradstreet, in "To My Dear Children," feels it important to leave her descendants a record of her struggles to accept the dictates of Puritan theology, struggles that her poetry shows to have been life-long. For Margaret Cavendish, author of the first secular autobiography by a woman, the "other" was her husband, the Duke of Newcastle, whose biography she wrote several years after she wrote the *True Relation of My Birth, Breeding and Life*. Mason's point is not that these women efface or subordinate themselves to the "other," but rather that self-definition is for them relational instead of purely individual.

Allied with this relational self-concept is the fact that women's autobiographies emphasize the network of familial and other personal relationships that they regard as essentially formative and nurturing, not merely in early life but throughout the life cycle. Once Benjamin Franklin, in his *Autobiography*, has recounted his rejection of the career choices and apprenticeships selected for him by his father and older brother, he leaves behind mention of family to concentrate on his individual accomplishments in the public sphere; but women's autobiographies as disparate as Margaret Halsey's *No Laughing Matter: The Autobiography of a WASP*, Maxine Hong Kingston's *The Woman Warrior*, and Virginia Woolf's *Moments of Being* circle back again and again to their relationships with parents, friends, and lovers. Whereas the male autobiographer tends to see such relationships as a stage in development to be left behind once one has achieved an individual autonomy, women view them as dynamic, evolving parts of life, subject to revision, redefinition, and often reconciliation—especially the relationship between mother and daughter. As the studies reported in Carol Gilligan's *In a Different Voice* show, women are inclined to make decisions in the context of relationships, whereas men more frequently do so according to rules and hierarchies.

A related characteristic of women's autobiography is the tendency of women who have had remarkable careers and been prominent public figures to focus in their life stories on the private, domestic parts of their lives. As Heilbrun points out, Jane Addams, Ida Tarbell, and Margaret Mead tend to treat their vocations as accidental or incidental to the personal lives that they foreground in their texts, and she proposes the reason for this as the conflict that women have felt between the two lives; when presenting themselves to the public, they may have unconsciously downplayed their public accomplishments in favor of the socially-sanctioned domestic self. Such tensions have typically not affected men's lives, Heilbrun notes:

> We hardly expect the career of an accomplished man to be presented as being in fundamental conflict with the demands of his marriage and children; he can allow his public life to expand occasionally into the private sphere without guilt or disorder. These women are therefore unable to write exemplary lives: they do not dare to offer themselves as models, but only as exceptions chosen by destiny or chance. (25)

The frequent mention and exploration of physical or mental illness is a thematic thread that forms yet another characteristic of women's autobiography. Often, as with Alice James, Charlotte Perkins Gilman, Virginia Woolf, and Maxine Hong Kingston, physical disability is closely tied to or is the result of mental or emotional disturbance; the women skirt or succumb to "hysteria" or insanity. In some cases, the stress produced by the tension between public and private demands or aspirations can be identified as the source of the illness—the most dramatic instance being Gilman's autobiographical story "The Yellow Wallpaper," in which enforced idleness (S. Weir Mitchell's famous "rest cure") proscribes a woman's freedom to write and thus exacerbates rather than alleviating her condition. Physical or mental weakness is not only a counterpart of behavioral passivity; it becomes a metaphor for powerlessness. Ironically, such disability may also be a woman's perverse claim to individual identity, as when Alice James, a life-long invalid, writes in her diary that her "glorious role was to stand for *Sick headache* to mankind!"[9] Being immobilized by illness may also be regarded as restorative rather than merely restrictive by women autobiographers. By 1930, for example, Virginia Woolf was able to regard her debilitating headaches as periods of gestation for her writing. "I believe," she writes, "these illnesses are in my case—how shall I express it?—partly mystical. . . . my mind . . . becomes chrysalis."[10] The mysterious illness that afflicts the narrator of Kingston's *Woman Warrior* in adolescence is described as a welcome interlude in a difficult childhood: "It was the best year and a half of my life. Nothing happened."[11]

Rachel Maddux's *Communication* has much in common with these general patterns and themes in women's autobiography, and, like so much of women's autobiographical writing, it defies strict genre definition. It begins and ends as a letter "to and for dear John," and like a letter it is dated: September 17, 1941. The intended recipient is addressed as "you" intermittently in the text, sometimes in an accusatory tone and finally with gratitude and affection. There is evidence that the manuscript was actually sent to John, but it remained a piece of private correspondence, so it exists as a previously unpublished memoir. Further, Maddux declares her freedom from any requirements of form in the preface to *Communication* when she asks, "Why should I not meander? Why should I not take pleasure in the telling?"

In some senses, John functions as the "other." Not only is he invoked as the "you" of the text, but he has instigated the writing of the text itself by refusing to hear Maddux's story in person. Maddux's language in the preface suggests that this refusal had two origins. The first is that the hearing might seem to have suggested an emotional commitment that John was reluctant to make, which Maddux counters by maintaining, "I would never cast upon you more than you could wear with ease." The second reason for his reluctance to hear her out seems to be an inability to take her youthful explanation of her life seriously, for she asks, "Why should you deny the validity of my find? What has this to do with age?" Whatever the reasons for his refusal to listen to her story in person,[12] John's suggestion that she write down the story of her search for communication resulted in a manuscript of just over a hundred double-spaced pages. Yet unlike the writers to whom Mason refers in "The Other Voice," who achieve a general sense of selfhood in relation to the "other," Maddux neither seeks nor derives validation of her personhood; rather, she gains a specific sense of herself *as an author* by writing to John. In the last paragraph of *Communication* she relates the writing of her autobiography to her future writing:

> By writing this to the only person in the world who could understand ALL of it *the way it is said*, I think I have learned how to write so that later things can be understood by any human being who has breathed the air in and breathed it out and learned to read and asked himself one question.

After reading *Communication* one doubts not the sincerity but the accuracy of Maddux's statement that John was the "only person in the world" who could understand it, because her experiences and the manner in which she tells of them resonate with other women's lives and their accounts of them, a circumstance made far more clear in 1991 than it was in 1941 by the intervening years of feminist scholarship.

Maddux's relationship with her mother, for example, follows a now-familiar pattern of separation and reconciliation. Her desire for the attention of her difficult, temperamental father deflected attention away from her mother, and her mother's attitude that "there was something weak about poor health" made it impossible for Maddux to confide in her about the childhood headaches. (Even aspirin was withheld from her; Maddux reports that when she later discovered that aspirin could dull her headaches she was "mad all through" at the realization that this simple form of relief had been denied by her mother.) Indeed, much of what Maddux recounts about her childhood relationship with her mother centers on health. When she complains of back pains, her mother takes her, out of ignorance, to an inept chiropractor, who compounds the problem; the only way Maddux can avoid further visits is to tell her mother that her back is better—and the lie increases the distance between them. As is the case with her other problems, both physical and emotional, Maddux must seek her own solution to the back problem, and like Woolf and Kingston, she finds the enforced idleness of her recuperation beneficial: "I could not wish for a creative child a greater blessing than a serious illness before twenty. A time of contemplation and of QUIET is essential to the flowering . . . ." Much later in her life, in a letter to a friend who had had a serious illness, she writes, "After the emergency subsides, I've always found convalescence a very productive period and I hope you will, too."[13]

When Maddux later lists those with whom she has attempted to achieve true communication, the list includes her father and her sister—and even her imaginary playmate, Tawm—but it does not include her mother. It is only after Maddux has moved away from home, become involved with an older man, and experienced a pregnancy that she forces her mother to tell her own story and thus begins to see life from her perspective.

The emphasis in the chapter "My Mother" on the extremes of silence and communication bring to mind a similar emphasis in more recent fiction and autobiography by women—notably, Alice Walker's *The Color Purple* and Maxine Hong Kingston's *The Woman Warrior*, both of which open with parental admonitions to silence, and both of which testify to the ability of language to empower women. But in addition to resonating outward to the work of other writers, the mother-daughter relationship in *Communication* is also closely related to other themes within the autobiography itself, such as Maddux's desire to have a child, and her need to be taken seriously on her own terms—which defines the search for what she calls "communication." Alice Miller's *The Drama of the Gifted Child*, a study of the loss of the creative, authentic childhood self because of parental demands and expectations, offers some insights into these related themes. Miller, a psychoanalyst who practices in Switzerland, believes that all children—but especially gifted children, among whom we must surely count Rachel Maddux—need to be able to develop a "healthy narcissism":

> The child has a primary need to be regarded and respected as the person he really is at any given time, and as the center—the central actor—in his own activity. In contradistinction to drive wishes, we are speaking here of a need that is narcissistic but nevertheless legitimate, and whose fulfillment is essential for the development of a healthy self-esteem.[14]

As Maddux recounts her desire to have her own child in *Communication*, shortly before she becomes pregnant, she uses almost the same language as Miller: "the child should never live on any standards but its own." Her wish for a child is clearly linked to a need to reverse the pattern of her own upbringing; in the same passage, she asserts that "when the child spoke to me I would not turn my back to it and rattle pans," using almost precisely the same language as in her later accusation to her mother: "you turned your backside to me and rattled pans when I came to tell you of my great theories."

This sense that Maddux's desire for a child stems at least in part from an attempt to revise her own childhood is reinforced by the fact that much earlier in *Communication*, when Maddux is about seven, she kills her imaginary playmate (Tawm, who lives in a rosebush) and instead imagines an actual baby, at about the same time that her childish questions ("What makes a train go?" "Why can't the cat talk?") are being met with insincere, inattentive responses. Maddux's remarks in *Communication* about imagining having a real baby are amplified in the story "Mother of a Child," published in *Story* in 1938. The little girl in the story has an "abnormal passion for maternity," and goes through an imaginary nine-month pregnancy. The importance of early childhood experience to Rachel Maddux is also underscored by its presence as a thematic element in her other published work: Erma's fervent longing to raise a child in *The Green Kingdom*, for example, and the account of Maddux and her husband's unsuccessful attempt to adopt two children in *The Orchard Children* (1978).

Alice Miller's work with adults whose authentic feelings were not attended to in childhood also bears upon the central theme of Maddux's autobiography: the search for "communication with a human being, for the recognition of someone who was *attentive* to the same things *in the same way*, for another mind that could not fool itself." The feelings and perceptions that are not nurtured and developed constitute a self-concept that becomes buried, overlaid by the emotions and responses "accepted and approved by their inner censor, which is their parents' heir" (21). The true self remains in what D. W. Winnicott terms "a state of non-communication" because of its need for protection (20). What is remarkable about *Communication* is that Rachel Maddux describes the actual process of burying this "true self" in the form of eradicating her fears and emotions. In the chapter titled "Self-Sufficiency" she tells of how, at the age of ten, she "abandoned the search for communication in an extraordinary struggle for self-preservation." Already, at the age of ten, experiencing the depression that afflicts Miller's patients in adulthood, Maddux sets about to conquer the emotional states that she associates with her depressive episodes.

It is significant in the context of women's autobiography that the responses Maddux feels she must deny are those that we identify particularly with the cultural construction of the "feminine." The list, as she presents it, is as follows:

1. crying in the movies
2. feeling sorry for people

3. feeling affectionate and having no outlet for it, as to my father or my sister
4. getting excited
5. trying to explain something and not being able to.

It is the emotional, affective, inarticulate, *female* self that must be expunged—that Maddux identifies as the source of her "insanity." She must conquer "the headaches and the need of people." Having identified the cause of her headaches as her various fears, she sets out systematically to overcome those fears. As rationally as Benjamin Franklin devising a scheme for achieving moral perfection, Maddux arrives at a plan to destroy her fears and emotions: "I only had one method and I worked it on one of them at a time until I could pass a fear test and then I would cross that one off my list." The process lasts six years, until finally Maddux can state, "I was afraid of nothing. I felt nothing." The self that remains is pure intellect; Maddux describes herself from the ages of seventeen to nineteen as clear-headed and in perfect control: "I could get along without anything or anybody and I would be sane too."

Maddux's decision to reject her female-identified emotional self in favor of her male-identified intellectual self reverses the traditional premise that underlay S. Weir Mitchell's "rest cure"[15]: that engagement in intellectual activity was debilitating to women, and could even lead to madness. As Gilman undercuts this premise in "The Yellow Wallpaper," showing a woman driven mad by the lack of mental stimulation, so Maddux chooses the intellect as her path to sanity. In so doing, she marks her distance from Alice James, who reports in her *Diary* her retreat from intellectual activity, "absorbing into the bone that the better part is to clothe oneself in neutral tints, walk by still waters, and possess one's soul in silence"(95). Maddux's is a different isolation; cut off from the emotive, relational part of herself, she feels freed to pursue mental endeavors traditionally identified as masculine.

After two years of this hard-won self-sufficiency, however, Maddux realizes that it is not a "great, free, sunlit meadow," but rather a "deep well with a high wall around it," and in an effort to end her isolation she enters into a series of relationships with men that become abusive. Attracted by her cool, detached demeanor, men were determined to break down her coldness and make her feel—"even anger." With no understanding at the time of why she attracts "crazy people," Maddux is beaten and otherwise abused many times until she finally realizes that it will take her a long time to learn to feel again, so thoroughly has she submerged this ability. It seems no accident that when she finally does fall in love it is with a man thirty years her senior who considers the age difference too great for marriage. Indeed, the most important aspect of the relationship, which had lasted ten years by the time *Communication* was written, is that by allowing her once more to feel, he removed her from her self-imposed isolation; as Maddux tellingly puts it, "He gave me back my childhood."

It is with this man—who remains nameless—that Maddux conceives the child that does not live. Her search for communication renewed, she wills the pregnancy, as she had done imaginatively in childhood, so that she can give a child the attention she did not have. Whether the pregnancy ended in abortion or stillbirth is unclear from the text, and neither word is ever used.[16] Maddux writes of being "gloriously" happy in her pregnancy; she refers to the child as a "son," speaks of being hospitalized, and says that she is sorry that her son will not "see the green things growing in the spring." All of this, plus the lack of easy access to abortion in the 1930s, suggests a stillbirth or a death in early infancy. Yet there is no physical description of the child, and Maddux notes at one point that "it was wicked to ask a child to do for you what you cannot do for yourself," suggesting that she might have realized in time for an abortion that she had become pregnant for the wrong reasons. There is little concrete detail in this section of the autobiography, whether because of Maddux's reluctance to be fully candid about the episode or because the actual details are less important than her realization that her maternal feelings exist for any warm-blooded creature—feelings that re-emerge in Erma's love for the feathermanes in *The Green Kingdom* and Libby Meredith's love for the goats in *A Walk in the Spring Rain* (1966).

As much as such themes and incidents place *Communication* in the tradition of women's autobiography, however, the story of her life that Rachel Maddux tells at twenty-eight differs from other texts in that tradition in striking ways, most of which are prefigured in her subtitle: *Being the Mental Autobiography of a Sturdy Quest.* This subtitle, which has the ring of an eighteenth-century book title, places the emphasis on intellect and strength— qualities not traditionally associated with women. If an autobiography is in part an exercise in self-definition, *Communication* locates that definition in the strength of the mind—a "mind that could not fool itself," as Maddux writes. The image that emerges is of a woman willing to confront herself, one who seeks essences in herself as well as in the rest of the world.

The best example of self-confrontation—though by no means the only one—is the sequence in which Maddux determines to conquer her emotions. The passage in which she decides that she must take action is worth drawing attention to in its entirety because of the sharpness of its language:

> I was ten years old and it was early morning. Our house faced west and the house itself cast a cool shadow which reached almost to the sidewalk. Here the shadow made a sharp line. So must this day make a sharp line for me. No more must I go blundering about, crying and having headaches and reaching and not finding and leaving things unexplained. This day I must act. I must save myself from insanity while there was yet time. Nobody could do this for me. I and my insanity were all alone there together, face to face, in the shadow of the early morning and we were going to fight it out.

The sharp line of the shadow is like a line drawn in the dirt that she dares herself to cross in order to take control of her life. Dependent on no one else—"nobody could do this for me"—she cross-examines herself, forcing honesty, refusing to allow her mind to fool itself. A few paragraphs later she notes that during this "brutal" conversation with herself she was sharpening a knife on the wood of the steps—metaphoric preparation for battle with the forces of what she believes is insanity.

Other episodes in *Communication* show Maddux confronting others for the sake of what she believes in. The most dramatic of these occurs when, in high school, she defends a classmate who is accused of being a lesbian following the suicide of the young woman she is assumed to have been involved with. Such an accusation in Wichita, Kansas, in the 1920s was not only shocking, but was accompanied by a great deal of ignorance; the townspeople even confuse the terms "homosexual" and "hermaphrodite." In trying to understand why, as a teenager, she understood homosexuality herself, Maddux recalls that a little girl she had played with years before was a lesbian: "Everything she did and said seemed very logical FOR HER and I had simply accepted it." What this statement and others throughout *Communication* reveal is Maddux's firm belief that identity is inherent in the individual and cannot—and should not—be conferred by others on the basis of gender, sexual preference, skin color, or any other characteristic. This unquestioning acceptance of people as they are would later inform her story of a friendship between a white woman and a black woman in *Abel's Daughter* (1960).

Maddux's rigorous search for *essences* brings her to direct confrontation with the issue of selfhood that is at the heart of the autobiographical enterprise. Early in her childhood, she both recognizes the power of language and also learns to distrust language as a sufficient indicator of the essential nature of things and people. Maddux records in *Communication* her realization of the authority of the written word when she helped secure the pardon of a chicken thief by writing to the governor of Kansas: "This writing, I thought, is a serious thing, and not to be fooled around with."[17] But the spoken word she finds less reliable. When she asks her parents why a chair is called a chair, she is told, "because you sit in it"; not satisfied, Maddux writes, "I called it a flower and sat in it to see if it would hold me up." She longs as a child for the day when essences would be revealed to her:

> I would look at an oak tree then and it would slowly change from being a member of a group of trees to being this tree. It would shimmer all over and come to life, the way trees do in Walt Disney's cartoons, and it would show me its oakness and I would show it my rachelness.

It is Maddux's unswerving certainty that there is an essential "rachelness" that sets *Communication* apart from most autobiographical texts by women,[18] which are characterized by what Shari Benstock terms "female discontinuity"[19]—a hesitancy about self-definition, a distrust of memory, an unwillingness to assert a coherent self. Instead, Maddux's autobiography more nearly conforms to the concept of autobiography that Benstock identifies with the Western male tradition:

> The self appears organic, the present the sum total of the past, the past an accurate predictor of the future. This conception of the autobiographical rests on a firm belief in the *conscious* control of artist over subject matter; this view of life history is grounded in authority. (19)

It is precisely the authority of the author's voice that marks *Communication.* For all that we must regard all autobiography as invention, and to that extent fictive, this author, who announces herself to be "absolutely confident that she will some day write a great book," claims the right to "do [herself] justice"—and convinces us that she has somehow done so.

2. "The only Bohemia in town"

When Rachel Maddux completed *Communication* in September of 1941, she was living in an apartment at 16 West 43rd Street in the Westport section of Kansas City, Missouri. Having graduated from the University of Kansas and spent two years in medical school, she held a series of odd jobs while attempting to establish herself as a writer. On the balcony of the apartment Maddux grew

herbs and "all kinds of strange flowers,"[20] and the apartment itself was a gathering place for writers and would-be writers. Having
achieved a measure of recognition with the publication of *Turnip's
Blood*, Maddux, in her mid-twenties, was at the center of Kansas
City's literary activity in the years immediately preceding
America's entry into World War II. The description by Kansas
City journalist Martin Quigley to which Susan Wiltshire refers in
her foreword emphasizes Maddux's physical attractiveness and
her generous encouragement of other writers:

> She was a beautiful Junoesque young woman with long reddish-blonde
> hair. A reclusive mystic with a slow sweet smile, she was wise and
> gifted and made us feel wise and gifted. Her apartment, whose only
> other permanent resident was a big black dog that must have had a
> name, became a haven for the great issues of the day that were swirling
> us into their vortex. We were all writers of sorts and we talked more
> about writing than anything in the outside world. Rachel commanded
> that we publish our own literary periodical to be called *Here and Now*.
> We all wrote things—stories and essays and poems—and Rachel was
> kind about them and gave them gentle readings. But *Here and Now*
> became there and then before the first issue went to press. Rachel
> wrote her first novel, *Turnip's Blood*, in that apartment. It was the only
> Bohemia in town. [21]

Quigley's characterization of Maddux as "reclusive" seems odd in
light of her conduct of nightly salons for young writers, but it is
likely that he perceived that she withheld parts of her life—most
notably, her relationship with a man thirty years her senior—
from even those with whom she was in frequent contact.

If Maddux could be regarded as reclusive, she was also capable
of sudden enthusiasms and impetuous behavior. Her first meeting
with Savington Crampton, which developed into a life-long
friendship, provides an example. In the early summer of 1937, on
his way to California from Bucks County, Pennsylvania, to take
over production of the "Camel Caravan" radio program, Crampton
made a detour to Kansas City to meet the author of *Turnip's
Blood*, which he had read in *Story* magazine. Arriving in Kansas

City at 11:30 a.m. on Sunday, June 20, Crampton and his traveling companion, script writer George Corey, found Maddux's apartment and spent the rest of the day with her; when they left at 5:15 p.m., Maddux left with them, traveling to their next stop in Chapman, Kansas, where the three of them spent the night. The next morning, Crampton and Corey headed west toward Denver, and Maddux took the train back to Kansas City.[22]

What is it about *Turnip's Blood* that caused a radio producer to seek out its author? In *Communication* Maddux writes of hearing "words spoken out loud" and writing them down to get the voice out of her head, until "when the voice did not come back anymore that was the end." The story has some of the quality of a dream, even though nothing in it is outside the realm of the possible. A fifty-year-old physician, out at dawn after a late night emergency, meets a young woman sitting on a park bench. Though she has been through four years of college, she scrubs floors in his office building and is oddly child-like: when the doctor asks her fondest wish, it is to have her dog trained to eat at the table with her, and after several weeks she goes off to join a traveling circus.[23] A serious accident at the circus destroys her ability to walk, and the doctor, a widower, marries her as a means of taking care of her. The difference in age between the two central characters suggests that the story was inspired by the relationship with an older man that Maddux describes in *Communication*, and just as this man gave Maddux back her childhood by reawakening her authentic emotions, so David Lawrence, the doctor in *Turnip's Blood*, is fascinated by and in many ways encourages the child-like qualities of Eve. With the aid of a specially-designed brace, he does train Rameses the dog to sit at the table, and after he and Eve are married he reads fairy tales to her at night. Most telling of all is the ending of the story, when David comes home to find Eve crying uncontrollably because, in her words, "I think I'm growing up."[24]

The theme of needing to keep one's childlike aspects is common to not only *Communication* and *Turnip's Blood* but also an unpublished short story that was also written during Maddux's years in Kansas City.[25] Titled "Change," the story, set during World War II, concerns a pregnant young woman whose husband is in the Navy overseas, and a young boy who continues to fail the first grade because he does not want to leave his first-grade teacher. As Eve, after her marriage to David, creates in the attic a replica of the apartment in which she lived when they met, so the boy in "Change" wants to keep his life the way it is. Amy, the pregnant woman in "Change," has different but no less compelling reasons for desiring stasis: she has not heard from her husband for three months, and lives with a barely-suppressed fear that something has happened to him. Amy's own anguish enables her to understand the boy's fear of a new second-grade teacher. These three works are linked also by the theme of creativity. Eve, in *Turnip's Blood*, has talent as a sculptor, carving a replica of David's hands out of wood. She is also an imaginative storyteller who amuses David with invented accounts of her day's activities when he comes home from work. Buddy, the boy in "Change," is able to recreate with convincing grace the actions of playing basketball with neither basket nor ball: "So real was the pantomime that long afterwards when Amy remembered the scene, she remembered the sound of the ball hitting the floor."[26] So content is Buddy with his imaginary game that he does not ask his parents to give him a real basketball.

The creativity that characterizes Maddux's childhood in *Communication* takes forms other than writing; the child that Maddux describes in her autobiography is concerned with distinctions between time and space, with devising ways to conquer her physical and emotional problems—in short, with coming to terms with the realities that surround her sensitivities. Not only does she not mention writing as a child or young adult; but when she begins to describe the origins of *Turnip's Blood*, she writes, "I was not writing, was not studying writing, was not thinking about writing, never meant to write." Yet later in her life, Maddux recalled that as a child she wrote a novel and showed it to the father of a friend, who read it and complimented her on it. Further, she recalled that as an adult returning to her childhood home in Wichita, she found many of her childhood writings hidden in the house.[27] Whether Maddux had forgotten about her earlier writing at the time she wrote *Communication*, or whether in shaping her life in the autobiography she wanted to emphasize the manner in which *Turnip's Blood* came to her unbidden, it is difficult to determine at this distance; but it is significant that she is embarrassed when asked how she wrote the story because the "voice" she heard tell it might seem to be an "hallucination," and her art the product of her illness—"the awful, stupid way that I had heard people explain Van Gogh's painting entirely by his epilepsy." Having earlier been afraid that she was insane because of her "attacks," Maddux did not want her readers to think that her writing was the product of madness.

Although *Turnip's Blood* may have been inspired by events in Maddux's own life,[28] it contains elements of mystery that foreshadow some of her later work. The character Eve, like Eve in the Garden of Eden, seems to come from nowhere, to have no background. When David first encounters her on the park bench, he thinks she may be a prostitute, and suspects that his hunch is correct when Eve says that she has left her family. "Were they mean to you?" he asks, but is told that on the contrary they were very nice, but that Eve was "restless. They talked too much." Later, after Eve's accident, David suggests that she will have to go back to her family, but she refuses—"they'd make me work crossword puzzles, trying to keep me busy, and they'd be everlastingly sorry"—and instead suggests that David marry her. Just as Eve does not explain her family background, neither does she explain why she does not have a degree after four years of college, except to say that one had to be present at commencement, and she "couldn't bear the thought of it." Eve's desire for Rameses to be trained to eat at the table is the unexplained whim of a child, and there is no sign of her roommate, Alice, who supposedly occupies the apartment only at night, when Eve is at work. The early-morning meals of bread and cheese and fruit that Eve and David share before she joins the circus seem to materialize out of nothing, like Eve herself.

In order to maintain the aura of mystery that surrounds Eve, Maddux wrote *Turnip's Blood* primarily from the point of view of David Lawrence; the reader knows what Eve does, to the extent that David knows this, but seldom knows what she thinks. It is as though Maddux wrote an imaginative version of her youthful affair with an older man from the perspective of her lover, knowing that there were parts of her that remained mysterious to him, in part because of the nature of the relationship. In the process, whether deliberately or not, she makes David, for all his kindness and generosity to Eve, something of a conventionally sexist male. When, for example, Eve announces that she has no plans or ambitions for the future, David is surprised that this annoys him:

> He knew that he had said a thousand times that ambition ruined women, and that he would love, just once, to find a woman who wasn't ambitious, and now that he had found her he was provoked. He had occasion almost weekly to comment unfavorably upon what he called the modern generation, yet when Eve refused to fit his idea of that very generation he was angry with her for it.

Later, when Eve refuses a wheelchair in favor of having David's servant, Anthony, carry her around the house, David is gratified by the repetition of the traditional male capitulation to the female's impractical wishes: "David was much amused, as he always was at the sight of male servitude to a female whim. He was always amused at any human trait supposed to be characteristically 'masculine' or 'feminine.'"

Such sentiments were not uncommon in 1937—nor, indeed, are they in 1991—but their major function in the story is not to raise issues of gender equality or stereotyping, but rather to underscore the contrast between Eve's childlike impulsiveness and David's role as the rational benefactor. He is described as "a man of considerable mental discipline" whose mind "was of that reasoning texture which makes of a geometrical theorem a pleasure";

in contrast, he describes Eve as "the purely emotional type." In addition to being traditional characterizations of gender difference, these descriptions also represent the two aspects of Rachel Maddux's nature that are shown to be in conflict in *Communication*. Having, at the age of ten, decided that emotion was her enemy, Maddux undertook the project of suppressing it; at the time she wrote *Turnip's Blood*, she had begun once again to allow herself to feel, and the story is an imaginative representation of the tension between reason and emotion that remained an issue in her life. *Communication* offers a further clue to the origins of *Turnip's Blood*. In the final chapter of her autobiography, Maddux refers to Budd Schulberg's inability to understand the sequence about the dog eating at the table. When John remarks to Maddux, "If you do not understand that, . . . you have never been lonely," she acknowledges—albeit obliquely—that her experience of loneliness had contributed to Eve's character: "And yes, I looked at you and I admitted it. To no one else in the world had I ever admitted it."

The combination of loneliness, impulsiveness, and mystery that characterizes Eve was not only appealing to readers, but sparked a series of attempts to transform the novella into a drama for stage or film. Soon after meeting Maddux, George Corey wrote a script based on the story, but was not successful in finding a producer. More than twenty years later, in a letter to Savington Crampton, Maddux wrote that a producer in New York named Marvin Leibman had contacted her about his interest in making "a sort of musical" of *Turnip's Blood*. "Every twenty years," Maddux writes, "there is a new crop of girls and, among them, there seems always to be the perfect Eve." Leibman had read the story some years before while stationed in Africa during World War II; haunted by it, he told Maddux that he was afraid to read it again lest his memory of it be faulty. When he found the story to be as he remembered it, he began searching for a writer to do the script. "He has had *50* copies mimeographed. These he has sent out to dramatists in the hope of finding one who will catch fire on it. I guess he is pretty serious about it. Wouldn't it be fun after all this time?"[29]

Turnip's Blood continued to stir interest for many years after its initial publication. A version of it was broadcast on radio in September of 1945, though without Maddux's prior knowledge or any financial remuneration. In her September 19, 1945, letter to her husband, King Baker, who was overseas, Maddux writes of her frustration on both counts:

> ... Turnip's Blood was broadcast last night. Ain't it hell to get the papers a day old? I never knew a thing about it. John called today and he thinks not only I should have known but I should have been paid and I suspect Whit Burnett[30] is once again lying at the bottom of the wood pile. Damme, I wish I had heard it.

Still later, in May of 1951, Maddux received an appreciative letter from a reader of the story. In her journal, The Record, for May 21, 1951, she notes that someone named W. T. T. Ward, of the Island Trading Company of Micronesia, had read *Turnip's Blood* and had written to Wichita State University for her address. "Aye, it gives one faith, it does. I suppose if people knew how much this meant to a writer they would do it all the time. At least you'd think other writers would do it for one another."

3. The Green Kingdom and the Salton Sea

Maddux's completion of *Communication* in September of 1941, while for her the source of great satisfaction, evoked quite a different reaction from King Baker, then her fiancé, who was stationed at Fort Leonard Wood, Missouri. Baker seemed dismayed that the project was finished, especially because it now seemed to belong solely to Maddux rather than to them both. "Strange isn't it," he wrote to her on September 21, "that I was thinking all the time of this thing as something of *ours*, something between us rather than as a thing of yours, especially and entirely *yours*." Such a reaction is perhaps not surprising in light of the intensity

of Maddux's attempt to communicate with another man—John—
and the description in *Communication* of her long affair with an
older man. At the end of this very long letter, Baker pleads for
Maddux's absolute fidelity to him. "When the time comes you
must be *mine*. I don't mean mostly or relatively. I mean *altogether*. Not that I am suspicious or jealous because by nature I am
not but I know now that I must have complete assurance that my
perfect love is reciprocated." Whether or not Baker ever received
from Maddux this "complete assurance," they were married in
Chicago on December 18, 1941; Baker was thirty-two, and Maddux had just turned twenty-nine. Baker was recalled into the
Army in 1942 and by June of 1944, with Baker in England, Maddux
had moved to Los Angeles, where she lived in an apartment
owned by Lorraine Noble, a script writer with whom she collabo-
rated on script versions of several of her stories.[31] That summer
she completed the story "The House in the Woods," which was
published in *Collier's* in February, 1945.

Two major dreams occupied Maddux during the next three-
and-a-half years of frequent moves and concerns for Baker's well-
being. One was the completion of the manuscript of *The Green
Kingdom*, which she had begun in Kansas City in 1941, and the
other was building a house near the Salton Sea east of San Diego.
Both dreams required enormous patience: *The Green Kingdom*
was not completed until 1953 (and not published until 1957), and
the house by the Salton Sea was never a permanent reality, because when Baker returned from overseas he was eager to work on
the engineering degree that the war had forced him to postpone.

Despite Maddux's resolve to devote herself to her novel, news
of the war and particularly her fear for the safety of Baker and
their friends who were also overseas were powerful distractions.
A postscript to her June 18, 1944, letter to Baker, marked "not to
be sent in the letter," concludes with the expression of her anxi-
eties: "this night I fear for your safety, desperately, frantically,
unreasonably." By August of 1944 Maddux was having to remind

herself that she was first and foremost a writer. A 43-page letter to Baker written on August 10 reveals a deep crisis of self-definition as she reflects on past and present options and choices. Facing, as did so many couples at the time, an uncertain post-war future in an era of increasing specialization, Maddux dwells in the letter on the distinction between "amateur" and "professional," between possessing certain skills and abilities and being certified by some external agency to practice them. Having reassured Baker that she will not be "nervous if you do not come home with a 'post war plan' all ready to start in 24 hours," she nonetheless wishes that he would return with "a determination to lose your amateur standing":

> I say this in the horrible bitterness of self-knowledge. . . . The brilliant, the talented children, what tragedy there is for us. There is no place for an amateur in this world. Once there was. Think how the word dilettante, the word amateur, how they were once *not* terms of derision, but great compliments, marks of distinction.

The two major ways in which Maddux had previously sought to define herself—as doctor and as mother—had been dissipated by circumstances largely beyond her control, primarily her health, but longing for both still lingered.

"Let me tell you," Maddux writes in this letter, "the awful bitterness it is to have spent six years studying to be a doctor and to find oneself in WARTIME, unfitted to be a nurse." She admits that she is "snobbish" enough that "since once I planned to be a doctor, I am too good to be a nurse," and recognizes that such a feeling is "stupid." There are some professions she feels no pressure to be "professional" about, such as teaching and stenography, because these have not been her goals; but she regrets not having received her credentials—what she calls her "button"—in medicine: "I never can say I did not want to be a doctor. I did. I failed. It is hard to believe." Motherhood, unlike medicine, is not closed off to her, but she is ambivalent about it. Remembering the aborted child, she writes, "It is possible I made a mistake, but I don't think so . . . for the good of the child, perhaps I never should

have one." Later in the letter Maddux writes about the possibility
of adopting children so that Baker will have a family to come
home to, but she worries about the interference with her writing:

> And the children. Well, my God are you going to raise children now or
> are you going to write The Green Kingdom. And if you are going to
> forsake the Green Kingdom for children, why the hell didn't you have
> one of King's. Better forget it. Better leave the children until after the
> staring [sic] period and GET ON WITH THE GREEN KINGDOM.

Like so many women, Maddux recognized that motherhood and
her profession would compete for her attention, possibly to the
detriment of both.

It is writing, Maddux keeps reminding herself, that is her profession:

> And how is it I feel a professional? Ah, I have my little button. I have
> been published. And yet I know that is the matter of the merest luck.
> You have only to look at what is published to know how little it
> means. But I think when G. K. is published I will feel that it means
> something. Oh, this is crap. Every time I write, while I write, I feel like
> a writer. I feel like a fine writer.

Maddux's expectations about the place of writing in her life have
been overturned by the war and the attendant need to earn money
while Baker is overseas. "Without the war," she writes, "I was all
set. I had it licked. My husband made the living. I could be an
amateur financially and a professional professionally." But faced
with the necessity to be a professional in the financial sense, and
knowing that it would be a long time before she finished *The
Green Kingdom*, she was forced to take a series of part-time jobs
and at the same time resented the energy this took away from her
true profession.

Earlier in her life, speaking about writing to a college audience,
Maddux was able to approach with optimism the issues that
produced so much conflict during the war years. Advising those
in her audience who were committed to writing not to let anything deflect them, she stated, "So long as you keep the right

hand for writing, it doesn't matter what you have to do with the left hand." Better able at this point, at least in public, to view writing as something that occupies one's professional attention but not necessarily all of one's time, she encouraged her listeners to do whatever was necessary to keep the writing going:

> Writing is and should be a full time job if you can make it, but if you can't make it without compromise, then you'll have to go to work, that's all. And what you have to do to eat, so long as it is not writing, hardly matters. . . . If you are on the road toward great writing, if you even think you're on the road, then it will not matter if you do housework in Kansas, because you will know that you're a princess in Oz.

But by August of 1944, after a series of unfulfilling jobs that served only to stave off poverty, such assurance was elusive. *The Green Kingdom* was still in the future, and the dream of a house by the Salton Sea seemed "long, long ago."

Complicating both the financial and emotional lives of Maddux and Baker during the early 1950s were their separate ordeals of waiting. For Maddux, the waiting concerned *The Green Kingdom*. As she finished each of the four volumes of the novel, she sent it to her agent in New York, Ann Watkins, who was trying to get the novel serialized in a magazine or dramatized for stage or television production. Ann's encouraging telegrams would be followed by silence that lasted for weeks. In May 1951, for example, Maddux reports in her journal that it is the 39th day of "no word about volume 3 of G. K. It does seem almost inconceivable that an agent and a publisher both in the business of handling writers could so treat a human being." Several years earlier, she had described more humorously the dreaded approach to the mailbox that most writers experience:

> How many times can a mailbox be approached with hope. Ah, an infinite number. The feet do slow down, it is true. After 5 or 6 weeks, they don't run. After 2 or 3 months they do drag a little. And then finally it is less real to see the envelope in the box than not to see it.[32]

Not knowing how long it would take for the novel to be published, Maddux was exultant when she finally completed the manuscript on December 14, 1953—fittingly, with music playing on the radio. She records that the book had been eighteen years in the making—"7 years of thinking and 11 years of writing"—and finishing the manuscript brought its own reward: "If I should die tomorrow, I feel that life and I are even. We do not owe one another anything more. I have had my heart's desire." But this feeling was difficult to maintain in the face of repeated rejections, and by June of 1954 she was in sufficient despair to write, "I hope to avoid dissolution, a nervous breakdown or suicide." More crushing than the fact that *The Green Kingdom* had not been accepted for publication is the lack of personal concern and sympathy from her agent and others who read the manuscript:

> A depression in fiction, especially in long fiction, I can accept. That people are not reading novels I know. That no one in publishing seems to have courage enough to gamble, that Ann W. is so woefully mistaken and changes with every comment—these things only really prove what the book is about, that the forces of sterility are ruling the world.[33]

In the spring of 1956, Simon and Schuster at last accepted *The Green Kingdom* for publication after requiring cuts in the massive manuscript that reduced it to 561 printed pages, roughly half of its original length. The manuscript, written in longhand in a number of notebooks, had been the major focus of Maddux's attention since 1941, and she later noted that through all the many moves that she and Baker had made during those years she had never lost a page of it. The publication of the novel in 1957 provoked a quite unexpected reaction: a man who owned a nursery on Long Island and had published a book on gardening two years before with the same title initiated a lawsuit against Simon and Schuster that was "causing quite a mess," as Maddux wrote to Savington Crampton. Efforts to sell the book to a film company failed, largely because of the expense of production, but Maddux was invited to speak to a number of book clubs and to the Pacific

Coast Writers' Conference in June of 1957. She found the experience rather bewildering, as she wrote to Crampton on May 22 of that year:

> Any help (HELP!) or advice on writers' conferences? I've never been to one, naturally, and in fact I don't understand why anyone goes or what it is they want or hope for. But I don't like to cheat them if I can help it.
>
> This whole business of interest in the personality instead of the product is really strange, isn't it? It's been a very educational experience for me.

In addition to being "educational," Maddux also found the experience of talking about *The Green Kingdom* "unhealthy," because it interfered with the production of new work: "You get to be like the mother of three who, at 40, is still talking of her debutante days."[34]

Just as Maddux "heard" the story of *Turnip's Blood*, so she heard the symphony that Justin Magnus is composing in *The Green Kingdom*. The four volumes of the novel—titled "Discovery," "Time of Innocence," "Time of History," and "The Fulcrum"—correspond to the four movements of the symphony, and the music came to her before the story. In her notes on the manuscript of the novel, Maddux describes this process:

> The Time of Innocence was, to me, the most satisfying of the volumes, that is, it most perfectly suited the music which preceded it. It was given to me to hear the four movements of Justin's symphony. Unfortunately I am unable to control or capture such experiences and, as the music fades from my memory, there is a feeling of terrible loss. The music for The Time of Innocence was very different from that of the other movements and, so far as I know, unlike any I had ever heard at that time.

Justin Magnus is the architect of the Green Kingdom in several ways. A concert tour has introduced him to the two young couples who accompany him on the quest for the kingdom, and it is his grandfather's map that leads them to the spot. Following his wife's suicide and a long illness, Justin, at the age of sixty, needs the renewal the kingdom seems to promise. Erma and Arthur Herrick, an idealistic young couple living in near-poverty, see the journey as a chance for a better life, while Joe and Gwen have serious doubts about the enterprise and create much of the conflict that occurs in the kingdom itself.

Several elements of *The Green Kingdom* echo themes established in *Communication*, most obviously the almost mystical relationship between Justin and Erma. In terms of the age difference between the two, the relationship parallels that between Maddux and her older lover and that between Eve and David in *Turnip's Blood*. At the end of *The Green Kingdom*, Erma, pregnant with Justin's child, lives on in the green world, Eve without Adam, content. The need for true communication is a thread in the novel as well. At the time that Justin meets Erma and Arthur, they are in the process of creating a record of the human experience by inviting as many people as will participate to write down the facts of their daily existence in notebooks. In the belief that any human life is valuable, they have embarked on the project known alternately as "The People's Library" and "The Human Records."[35] In the book that Arthur writes about the project, he notes that the rest of the natural world keeps an accurate history:

> The rocks keep an accurate record. Fossils hold facts. Calcareous strata and the rings of trees and the great loop-folded streams of lava know the value of the moment. Mankind, alone in nature, relies on retrospect.[36]

Maddux's search for the essential nature of people and things in *Communication* is given full rein in *The Green Kingdom*, when the five people must name the plants and animals of their new home and select names that refer to essential characteristics or functions. The result is animals named "feathermanes" and "ballsleepers," and plants called "greengrain" and "clusternuts."

4. *Abel's Daughter* and a Tennessee Orchard

The fantasy of an untouched world and the novel's insistence on the values of nurturance and mutual respect are consonant with other fiction that Maddux completed during the 1950s. Two of her stories were published in the magazine *Fantasy and Science Fiction*, and one of these, "Final Clearance," was included in *The Best From Fantasy and Science Fiction* in 1957. Long before *The Green Kingdom* was published, at least as early as the summer of 1954, she had begun work on a novel about a friendship between a white woman and a black woman in a small southern town in the 1940s. The novel is based in large part on her experience of living in Occoquan, Virginia, while Baker was stationed at Fort Belvoir, and for a long time she referred to it merely as "the Occoquan story." By August of 1957 she had completed the first eight chapters of the draft, and by the spring of 1958 she had chosen the title *Abel's Daughter*. Her agent attempted to interest a magazine in running the novel serially before showing it to Simon and Schuster. Neither the serialization nor the Simon and Schuster publication materialized, and Harper and Row published the book in 1960.

The narrator and central character of *Abel's Daughter* is Molly Demerest, a young Army wife innocent of racial prejudice who comes to know Serena, the daughter of Abel Loftis, a black man who runs a small grocery story in the town of Chinkapink. In a place and time of rigid segregation, Molly oversteps the boundaries of convention as she socializes freely with Serena Covington, gives her son books to read, and shops at Abel's store rather than at the "white" grocery. The white townspeople's attitudes toward blacks are epitomized by those of Lee Carter Higgins, who is restoring his family's former plantation, where slaves were bred for sale. Lee Carter believes that all blacks should be sent to Africa, and when Molly tells him that she must go back to town to prepare a school lunch for Serena's son while Serena is in the hospital, he is unable to see this as an obligation worth fulfilling: "The idea of taking a promise to a little nigger bastard seriously. . . . "[37] It is only when her husband is transferred and Molly is leaving Chinkapink that she learns the blacks in the community have been careful not to speak to her in public in order to protect her from white reprisals for her friendships with them. Molly and Serena correspond for years afterward, and the last letter in the book includes Serena's response to the 1954 school desegregation decision: "We have longed so long for equal education so our people can get decent jobs. But next September everything will be just the same that's what everybody knows, no matter what the Supreme Court say" (206).

At almost precisely the same time that *Abel's Daughter* was published early in 1960, Maddux and Baker were undertaking a major move: from Los Angeles to rural Houston County, Tennessee. For a number of years before this move—beginning with Maddux's dream of a house by the Salton Sea—they had devised ways of escaping temporarily from the urban environment. They made camping trips to the Salton Sea and to an area near Twentynine Palms and the Joshua Tree National Monument. In the early 1950s the couple homesteaded some land in the latter area, but were never able officially to lay claim to it. By 1957, the thirty-five-mile drive from their house in Tarzana to Baker's job had become a burden, and in the summer of that year they moved temporarily to an apartment in Los Angeles with a view toward a permanent move to the city.

But Baker had begun experimenting with growing fruit trees in Tarzana, a hobby that grew into the dream of owning an orchard. In August of 1957, Maddux wrote that they would leave the Los Angeles apartment to return to Tarzana in September, and "if the fruit trees die, King won't even speak to me."[38] About the same time, Katherine Brown, a friend of Maddux's from Kansas City days, and her husband bought 400 acres of land in Tennessee and named it The Green Kingdom; and by the summer of 1958 Maddux and Baker were thinking seriously of moving there:

There is room for all of us there, and running streams and plenty of rock and timber to build houses out of. . . . They plan a resort place, but have no capital and are having to do all their own labor, etc. Very rugged just now, but they're having a wonderful time. Anyhow King and I are going there on our vacation (don't know when yet) and have a look at it so King will believe it really exists when he wishes to leave Lansing. We might raise lilacs.[39]

The move to Tennessee took place in the winter of 1960. Baker went first and then sent for Maddux, her "thousands of pieces of paper," and her cat. Baker, who had planted 240 apple and peach trees before Maddux's arrival, looked to her "ten years younger" despite the fact that he had been forced to take a job at a nearby manufacturing plant to earn money to maintain the orchard. "But he is close to his beloved orchard and we will make out. . . . It is on a hill and is a very beautiful sight."[40]

Many of the details of the establishment of the orchard and the early years in Tennessee are contained in *The Orchard Children*, Maddux's only fully non-fiction work, which was published by Harper and Row in 1977. At the center of the book is the story of their hard-fought and ultimately futile attempt to adopt two foster children in the early 1960s, but here too is the story of an essentially urban couple becoming accustomed to a rural environment that required a great deal of self-sufficiency and determination. But, as Maddux writes, "we wanted to have a try at fighting nature instead of our fellow man, a battle for which we were both ill suited."[41] Having earlier yearned for an "anchored" life, Maddux approached the building of their house in the orchard with awe and some apprehension: "Would this be it, I wondered, the last home? There is always one house where you die" (44). Nearing fifty, and married for almost twenty years, Maddux also takes stock of her relationship with Baker. She thinks of "how essential it is for women (meaning me) to think they have made or can make some man happy, and how tenaciously we cling to this belief." When she enunciates this to Baker, he wonders whether she couldn't compromise to believe she had made someone "a

little less *unhappy*," but she cannot. "No, I could not compromise for something not good enough to have spent a life on. . . . If
I had a choice."

> But I did not really have a choice, I was thinking that New Year's
> Eve in the snow. For we were irrevocably committed to each other
> somehow. In sickness and health? That was the least of it. In grandeur
> or pettiness, wit or stupidity, fascination or screaming boredom, in
> truth or lies, meeting or worlds apart, drunk or sober, listening and
> deaf—we were committed.
>
> And now we were also committed to this land. (45)

This *would* be the last house Maddux would live in, and she and
Baker are buried in the orchard.

Although Maddux had several times mentioned the possibility
of adopting children, there is no evidence that she and Baker had
actively pursued adoption. Soon after they moved to Tennessee,
however, such an opportunity was quite literally brought to their
doorstep when the grandmother of a three-year-old boy and a five-
year-old girl asked Maddux and Baker to care for the children,
whose parents had abandoned them and were separated. None of
the members of the extended family spread over the hills of Houston County seemed willing or able to take the two children, so
Maddux and Baker agreed, and after a few months of caring for the
two frightened, malnourished children, they started adoption pro-
ceedings. But when the hastily—and, it turned out, temporarily—
reunited parents appeared, the court awarded them custody.

The experience of suddenly becoming a parent and just as
suddenly having that right taken from her was so painful that it
took Maddux many years to write *The Orchard Children*, and the
pain was in no way lessened by the knowledge that the children's
parents once again separated and brought the children back to the
very same grandmother, who was this time able to keep them.
But Maddux at least had the satisfaction of knowing that *The Orchard Children* brought to the attention of many people the flaws
in a child-custody system that did not have as its first concern the
welfare of the children themselves. This message reached even

greater numbers of people when the book was dramatized as a television documentary by CBS; retitled "Who Will Save the Children?" it starred Shirley Jones and Len Cariou,[42] and was aired in December of 1978.

A more immediate positive result of the months of foster care was the adoption of an infant girl in the spring of 1964. A young woman living in Chicago, who knew the parents of the two children that Maddux and Baker had cared for, called to say that she was unable to care for her daughter and wanted them to take her. Despite initial reservations regarding their age and Maddux's health, they agreed, and Melissa Ruth Baker, named for both of her grandmothers, came to live in the orchard. At the age of 51, Maddux was finally a mother. In describing Melissa's adoption in *The Orchard Children*, she makes a statement that echoes even in its language her concern in *Communication* that children be taken seriously. Noting that she still misses her two foster children, she writes, "One child does not take the place of another, of course. But the one you are looking at has a right to your very best attention" (245).

5. *A Walk in the Spring Rain*

Two years after Maddux and Baker adopted Melissa, Maddux's last novel, *A Walk in the Spring Rain*, was published by Doubleday. Just over 100 pages long, *Spring Rain* is her most perfectly controlled work of fiction; every word is precisely selected and placed in this spare volume. Yet the story is richly evocative and conveys deep emotion. The plot is simple, and in synopsis sounds almost clichéd. Libby Meredith accompanies her husband, Roger, to a rented farmhouse in West Virginia while he is on sabbatical from his position as a professor of law. He is to use the time to complete a book that is important to his career, and both of them will enjoy an environment vastly different from their native California. But Libby falls in love with Will Workman, a

West Virginia neighbor and local handyman, a gentle giant of a man who returns the feeling to such an extent that he kills his own son when he threatens Libby. The relationship is intense, but it ends abruptly when Libby and Roger learn that their daughter is ill and return to California.

Despite the story's potential for melodrama, Maddux avoids it, partly through the simplicity and candor of Libby's voice as she tells her story, and partly because of the convincing portrait of Will Workman. More than a love story, *A Walk in the Spring Rain* is, like most of Maddux's work, a novel about values—what is worth keeping and what is better left behind. Libby learns from Will to appreciate simple pleasures that are in stark contrast to her busy urban life: gathering watercress from a stream, caring for tiny Nubian goats, learning the names of plants. Most importantly, she learns about a kind of love so simple and direct and necessary that it exists outside time, age, and convention. Will asks nothing of Libby but to be allowed to love her, and the knowledge of his gentle, nurturing love becomes a talisman that she carries with her long afterward.

Certain elements of *A Walk in the Spring Rain* are clearly drawn from Maddux's own experience of moving from California to the eastern hill country. For a number of years in Tennessee she raised Nubian goats, a joy that she describes in *The Orchard Children*. Even Libby's early-spring discovery of watercress is based on an incident in Maddux's life; in one of her earliest letters from Tennessee, written in February of 1960, she describes "washing a carload of it free from pieces of oak leaves caught in the roots in order to get one small salad bowl full" to break the monotony of the ever-present cabbage offered locally.[43] As in *The Green Kingdom*, music is an important thread in this novel. In the prologue, in which Libby is observed walking from the market to her daughter's house, the complexity of a musical composition becomes a correlative for the contrast between her surface equanimity and the underlying concern for her daughter and longing for Will Workman:

If you were to set her to music, now, on this walk to Ellen's house. . . ,
why you would have a pleasant enough melody to begin with. . . .
moving in a brisk, healthy tempo. . . . But somehow there would begin
to intrude, beneath the pleasant melody, the quite incongruous note of
a bassoon (or, really, wasn't it more like a cello?) that would almost, at
first, be buried. Yet somehow, insinuatingly, it would prevail and
endure and gradually increase until it had swallowed everything else.[44]

The prologue, with its external, cinematic view of Libby, suggests
Maddux's earlier experience with writing filmscripts, and a version of it was retained when the novel was made into a film in
1969 with Ingrid Bergman and Anthony Quinn in the central
roles.

This was not the first time that Ingrid Bergman had been
interested in Maddux's work. In 1944, even before Maddux and
Baker moved to California, Bergman had read the filmscript of
Emmy Foster.[45] She read *A Walk in the Spring Rain* when it was
first published, and liked it very much. She recalls in her autobiography that she "thought it was wonderful finally to get a story
where the woman is fifty, and the husband is fifty-two, and she
falls in love with a man who might be older still."[46] Writer-pro-
ducer Stirling Silliphant had also been an enthusiastic reader of
the novel, and the final filmscript was the result of collaboration
among the three of them. The details of the transformation of the
novel into the film are recounted in Neil D. Isaacs' book *Fiction
into Film,* which contains the text of the novel, the filmscript,
and a record of the stages in production. After Bergman agreed to
do the film, in the fall of 1968, Silliphant sent Maddux a copy of
his script, and she responded with fifteen pages of notes under the
headings "human considerations," "picayune," and "landmarks
of the environment," according to Isaacs.[47] Some of her sugges-
tions were followed and others were not, but she was consulted
on several matters of authenticity. She allowed Annie Workman's
pie to be changed from wild blackberry to chess, but not to mince,
for example, and insisted that the word "maintenance" would
never have appeared on Will's business sign, so it was changed to

"fix-it." As soon as she heard that Bergman had agreed to do the film, she decided that the news justified her "going ahead and trying to buy some goats of the right age and color,"[48] which she intended to train for the film, not realizing that there would have to be two sets of goats of different ages.

Most of the differences between Maddux's novel and the film were necessitated by the switch from a narrative focus limited to Libby's perspective to the external eye of the camera. Roger, who is barely present in the novel, is far more fully developed in the film, and some of the development is based on Maddux's writing. When she was having difficulty placing the novel with a publisher, one editor suggested that she lengthen the novel and write it from a third-person perspective. Although loathe to abandon her original conception of the book, Maddux did complete four chapters of the revised manuscript (which was until its publication titled "The Human Condition"), and some of this material was used by Silliphant to enlarge Roger's role in the story. The urban location was changed from California to New York City, and the rural setting from West Virginia to—interestingly enough—Tennessee, and part of the film was shot in Knoxville, where the film premiered in April of 1970.

As Neil Isaacs notes in *Fiction into Film*, each person connected with the making of the film had somewhat different criteria for determining whether it was successful: financial profits, artistic coherence, individual performances. For Maddux, the central concern was how well the film conveyed her original vision—the music that she heard at its inception.[49] The film, as finally cut, was bitterly disappointing to her. One of the last cuts removed much of Bergman's walk in the rain that had originally opened the film (and that opens the novel and contributes its title); Maddux could not hear the music that she had written. Following the premier in Knoxville, she wrote a long, anguished letter to Ingrid Bergman, with whom she had developed a warm relationship during the production of the film. She had been pleased with Bergman's performance, but wondered if she knew what had gone wrong with the film. Bergman's response, written in France on May 25, 1970, is quite sympathetic to Maddux's concerns. The version she had seen earlier in Hollywood had retained the opening sequence, and she found the cut perplexing. "Maybe," she suggests, "Guy Green [the director] was afraid of sentimentality and that is dangerous in a picture. You have a lot of it in the book, but to me it is beautiful and moving. I think men are very frightened of it." Bergman thought the film might do well with the viewing public because "there are so many 'Libbys' in the world," and she is distressed by Maddux's disappointment:

> I hate the thought of having disappointed you. I who loved that book for so many years before it was made into a movie. It's sweet of you to think I personally have not betrayed you, but it must be so hard for you not to recognize "the music"!

Bergman continued to feel loyalty to Maddux's original conception and to regret her distress about the film. Ten years later, in her autobiography, she wrote, "We'd done our best and at the end of it we'd made Rachel Maddux cry."[50] The change from novel to film that could well have bothered Maddux more than anything else is Libby's reason for leaving Tennessee earlier than planned. In the novel, Libby learns that her daughter has cancer; there is no reasonable choice but to go to her. In the film, however, she leaves because Roger has become disillusioned with his work and wants to return to New York, so he assumes a centrality in her life that in the novel is occupied by Will.

6. "Dear friend, whoever you are, take this kiss"

After the initial struggle to get it started, Baker's orchard began to thrive. Maddux records in *The Orchard Children* the increasing numbers of bushels of apples—Lodi, Jonathan, Golden Delicious—and of peaches that they harvested and sold during the years when Melissa was growing up. They built a patio behind the small house from which they could see the fruit trees. Occupied with her daughter and the orchard, Maddux concentrated what time she had on writing *A Walk in the Spring Rain* and, finally, *The Orchard Children*. The orchard was not large enough to produce for a wholesale market; instead, like owners of other small orchards in north central Tennessee, Maddux and Baker ran a roadside business, waiting along the two-lane highway for people to stop to pick fruit or buy cider. Near the end of *The Orchard Children*, Maddux recalls one brisk day of sales when she began stuffing cash into a gallon jar after her cigar box overflowed; Baker saw the jar and remarked, "A whole gallon of money?" (247). Yet it was a precarious business, endangered by frost at the wrong time and all manner of insect life.

Two years after the publication of *The Orchard Children*, King Baker died of a heart attack on October 12, 1979. At his request, he was buried wrapped in a blanket in a plain pine casket. Maddux had assumed that because of her many health problems (which by now included emphysema), he would outlive her, and had already told him that she wanted to be buried "in the shade of a tree that would produce something edible so the squirrels would run up and down my arms, so to speak. . . . He was supposed to take care of my funeral. But here I sit, telling how I took care of *his*."[51] Taking care of Baker's orchard proved to be difficult for Maddux, whose recurrent bouts with the arthritis she had had since she was a young adult impaired her mobility, and late frosts in two successive springs destroyed the fruit crop. Maddux was increasingly forced to rely on financial assistance from friends, especially for such purchases as a heat pump for the house and a wheelchair.

Yet she kept her sense of humor, and she continued to write. In 1979, she began writing a play, then tentatively titled "The Last Man From Udall" and later titled "The Night the Clocks Stopped." "I don't think I have a talent for writing a play," she wrote, "or I would have been writing plays all this time. But still, what the hell?"[52] The play remained unfinished, but during the last two years of her life, she wrote a weekly column called

"Thoughts from a Country Orchard" for the *Buffalo River Review*, a newspaper published in Linden, Tennessee. Signing herself "Apple Annie," Maddux wrote warmly and often humorously about the progress of the orchard, and frequently reminisced about earlier parts of her life: a cricket cage bought in Los Angeles thirty years before, a childhood memory of the day the armistice was signed ending World War I, a toy farm that Baker had bought for her in Kansas City many years before, and, of course, Frances Voorhees. Never sentimental or melodramatic, the columns speak of human experiences that her Houston County readers could share. In the same column in which she writes with true anguish about the loss of the apple crop for the second year in a row, she tells of rescuing a bird that one of her cats had brought in: "What kind of fool would think she had made a significant gesture against a total crop failure by the restoration of flight to one chewed up bird?"

Yet it was natural for Rachel Maddux to put her own problems aside to attend to those of a bird, just as it was natural for her to search for Frances Voorhees and to adopt a child. Communication meant to Maddux far more than people understanding one another; it meant preserving the essentials of life and sharing them, as she offers a kiss in the quotation from Walt Whitman on her tombstone. The perfect and absolute communication that she describes in her autobiography is an ideal that she never stopped seeking. At times she was able to approximate it—with Erma and, briefly, with John—but primarily she tried to recreate it in her fiction: in the relationship between Libby and Will in *A Walk in the Spring Rain*, and between Justin and Erma in *The Green Kingdom*. Perhaps the goal of such a "sturdy quest" is to be found most certainly in fiction, or in a life that one creates for herself.

NANCY A. WALKER
Vanderbilt University

Notes to Introduction

1. *Story* 9, no. 53 (December 1936): 114. "Mother of a Child" was published in the April 1938 issue of *Story*, and "We Are Each Other's Children" appeared in the September–October 1938 issue.

2. There is evidence, however, that Maddux contemplated the possibility that *Communication* might be published in some form, though she never actively sought such publication. Shortly before she sent the manuscript to her close friend Savington Crampton in 1943, she was careful to distinguish it from her other work. "It is not a manuscript," she wrote; "it is a letter written to *one* person." Yet she also notes that, whereas the original had been written and sent in longhand, the recipient had returned it to her to be typed, urging her to "make a book of it." It was the typed version that she sent to Crampton. (Letter to Savington Crampton dated January 20, 1943.)

   The extant manuscript from which *Communication* is reprinted is an onion-skin carbon copy of the original typescript. This copy, long in the possession of Crampton, was given to Susan Wiltshire several years after Maddux's death, and is now among Maddux's papers at the Boston University library. The fact that she made a carbon copy and entrusted it to her dear friend "Savvy" suggests that she wanted it to be preserved among her papers. Further evidence that Maddux considered *Communication* a part of the canon of her writing is contained in correspondence between Maddux and King Baker, then her fiancé, who was stationed at Fort Leonard Wood, Missouri, during the time of its composition. In a letter to Baker dated September 18, 1941, Maddux writes:

   > I have treated you so badly this week and you have not had one decent letter from me, I know, but it was for a great cause. Now it is done and I am going to mail off the autobiography today and I think I will send it air mail special delivery just for the hell of it.

   The recipient of the original manuscript was a talent agent in Hollywood who worked primarily with writers for radio and film. For a brief period in the late 1930s and early 1940s, Maddux sent him manuscripts of some of her stories. Five years after sending him *Communication*, Maddux entertained serious doubts about whether she should have placed her trust in John. Several entries in her journal from the fall of 1946, when she was living in California and seeing John periodically, expresses disillusionment. On October 1 she writes:

> Did I make up the person to whom I wrote *Communication* in
> my own head? Was he always only an intellectual snob who cannot
> face competition in his own field and can only compete in a field for
> which he has no respect? This I would hate to believe. Was there not
> surely once a great heart there—a great understanding—a wonderful
> alertness?

3. Carolyn Heilbrun, W*riting a Woman's Life* (New York: W.W.
    Norton, 1988), p. 11.

4. If Maddux could carry this childhood argument into young adult-
    hood, she was also capable of sustaining friendships over long peri-
    ods of time. Early in *Communication* she writes of when, as a small
    child, she lost her friend Frances Voorhees "to space instead of
    time" when Frances' family moved away. More than sixty years
    later, Maddux wrote of this loss in a weekly newspaper column
    that she wrote for the *Buffalo River Review* in Linden, Tennessee;
    in the January 19, 1983, issue of the newspaper, Maddux reports
    that a New York reader had seen the column and sent her Frances
    Voorhees' address in Oregon, which allowed Maddux to begin a
    correspondence with her childhood friend.

5. Several years after completing *Communication*, Maddux again de-
    scribed graphically the symptoms of this disease that went undiag-
    nosed for so long:

    > It is so terrible when you are little and you do not have the
    > vocabulary for it and you do not know how to say that the design of
    > the wall paper seems to be in relief, and the red and green pencils in
    > the vest pocket of a man you pass on the street seem to you to be
    > imbued with special significance, that the world is too [sic] dimen-
    > sional, and that you find yourself full of tenderness for the uphol-
    > stery tacks in a leather chair. That you feel foolish and infuriated
    > and ashamed, and the possessor of special esoteric knowledge all at
    > once, and that you can hear the difference between linen and velvet.
    > (Letter to Savington Crampton dated September 19, 1944.)

6. Maddux began college in the fall of 1930 at Wichita State Univer-
    sity, where, with the exception of the spring semester of 1932, she
    attended for three years. In the fall of 1933, she transferred to the
    University of Kansas, where she received a B. A. degree in zoology
    in the spring of 1934. That summer, she began medical school at
    the University of Kansas; she withdrew in March of 1936.

7. Bella Brodzki and Celeste Schenck, eds., *Life/Lines: Theorizing
    Women's Autobiography* (Ithaca: Cornell Univ. Press, 1988), p. 1.

8. Mary G. Mason, "The Other Voice: Autobiographies of Women Writers," in James Olney, *Autobiography: Essays Theoretical and Critical* (Princeton: Princeton Univ. Press, 1980.)

9. Alice James, *The Diary of Alice James*, ed. Leon Edel (New York: Penguin, 1982), p. 48.

10. Virginia Woolf, *The Diary of Virginia Woolf*, Vol. 3, ed. Ann Olivier Bell (New York: Harcourt Brace Jovanovich, 1980), p. 287.

11. Maxine Hong Kingston, *The Woman Warrior: Memoirs of a Girlhood Among Ghosts* (New York: Vintage, 1977), p. 212.

12. In her journal (which she called "The Record") for October 9, 1946, Maddux suggests that one of the reasons might have been preoccupation with his own life:

> It seems strange to me that I, who have it to say, am always waiting around until it is convenient for the people I care for to listen to it. I think how John, newly married [for the second time], could not arrange a time to hear Communication (a joke of priceless irony) and asked me to write it. Few people are always ready for ideas.

13. Letter to Savington Crampton dated August 21, 1982.

14. Alice Miller, *The Drama of the Gifted Child: The Search for the True Self*, trans. Ruth Ward (New York: Basic Books, 1981), p. 7.

15. Silas Weir Mitchell (1829-1914) was a Philadelphia physician and author who developed a treatment of complete bed rest for women suffering from a variety of what were then termed "nervous disorders." Among those he treated were Edith Wharton and Charlotte Perkins Gilman.

16. Evidence outside the text suggests that the pregnancy ended in a stillbirth, although Maddux did have two abortions while in her twenties. Savington Crampton recalls helping her to find a doctor who would perform one in California in 1937, and that the father of the child was script writer George Corey, who worked with Crampton. The episode described in *Communication*—whether actual or invented—involves Maddux's Kansas City lover, and took place later. She definitely had an abortion in February of 1943, three months after she and King Baker were married. While the reasons for the first abortion have to do with the impossibility of a permanent relationship with the child's father, the reasons for the one in 1942 were more complex, and are detailed in a series of letters that Maddux wrote to Baker at Ft. Belvoir, Virginia, before and after the abortion. On February 15, the day after the pregnancy

was confirmed, she writes of her "cowardice," her fear of having the baby alone. But there were concerns about the health of Maddux and the child, too, primarily because of her *petit mal* epilepsy, so that the doctor (whose name Maddux did not reveal even to her husband) proceeded without waiting for the written approval from Baker that he ordinarily would have required. In a long letter to Baker, dated February 21, 1942, Maddux reports that she told the doctor, "I would not give this nervous system to a dog," and that he responded, "I think you are very wise." A statement in her February 25 letter to Baker confirms at least one earlier abortion; she has remarked to the doctor that she was surprised that the pain was so much greater than "the last time." By 1944, Maddux seems to have decided that bearing a child would be a mistake—"My God, if you had an epileptic how would you ever forgive yourself?"—and mentions the possibility of adoption. (Letter to King Baker dated August 10, 1944.)

17. This passage resonates with a similar passage in Mary McCarthy's *Memories of a Catholic Girlhood* (New York: Harcourt Brace Jovanovich, 1957, p. 63.) As a child in Catholic school, Mary wrote a couplet about the death of Pope Benedict, who was at the time "living, and, as far as I know, in good health"; when, a year later, the Pope indeed died, Mary had a "feeling of fearsome power, stronger than a priest's power of loosing and binding."

18. Maddux's recognition of individual identity—of her "rachelness"— brings to mind the lines in Elizabeth Bishop's poem "In the Waiting Room," when, three days before her seventh birthday, she comes to the realization of both her distinctiveness as an individual and her identity as a woman:

> But I felt: you are an *I*,
> you are an *Elizabeth*,
> you are one of *them*.

19. Shari Benstock, "Authorizing the Autobiographical," in Benstock, ed., *The Private Self* (Chapel Hill: Univ. of North Carolina Press, 1988), p. 20.

20. Letter to Savington Crampton dated September 3, 1938.

21. Martin Quigley, *Mr. Blood's Last Night* (St. Louis: Sunrise, 1980), pp. 113-14.

22. The dates and times are taken from a log-book that Crampton kept on the trip from Pennsylvania to California, noting mileage and the cost of gasoline for the trip in order to be reimbursed for his expenses.

23.   At one point, joining a traveling circus was a dream of Maddux's. In a sketch written for a composition class during her freshman year at Wichita State University, she describes two possible selves that she could become. One, whom she names Nana, is a free spirit who moves around as she chooses, at one point joining a "noisy carnival" where she stays "until she knows the life and desires of every freak and barker." The other self that Maddux imagines, named Ralleigh, is male, and plans his life carefully, working steadily to become a psychiatrist. Rachel concludes that she would like to be Nana for a few years and then become Ralleigh.

24.   Rachel Maddux, *Turnip's Blood*, in *The Flying Yorkshireman: Novellas* (New York: Harper & Brothers, 1938), p. 10.

25.   In a June 5, 1941, letter to King Baker, Maddux notes, "I think I will call the story Change. I like it better than Safety, I believe."

26.   Typescript of unpublished story titled "Change," p. 8.

27.   Mary Ann Gibson, "A Look at Rachel Maddux: A Talented and Successful Author," *Tennessee Magazine*, August 1980, p. 10. Several pieces of Maddux's earlier writing are among her papers at the Boston University library. At the age of eleven, she was awarded an honorable mention in a poetry contest sponsored by the *Scholastic Editor*, a national journal, and was the only junior high school student to be so honored. An early story titled "Self-sufficiency" contains elements that are echoed in *Communication*. A young mother, in her attempt to make her son strong, makes him into a cold, unemotional person who is ultimately completely dependent on others when he loses his eyesight.

28.   Conversations with Savington Crampton suggest that the story has strong autobiographical elements; he identifies Maddux's older lover as a Kansas City physician who was unable to obtain a divorce because of his wife's mental illness. In *Turnip's Blood*, Maddux more conveniently makes the male character a widower.

29.   Letter to Savington Crampton dated April 1, 1958. Leibman had somehow learned that George Corey had once written a script for *Turnip's Blood*, but Maddux was firmly opposed to Corey having anything to do with the project. She reports in the letter that she has told Leibman that "if I knew where [a script by Corey] was I would do nothing to bring it to anybody's attention." Despite this statement and her resistance to Corey's having any involvement in such a project, Maddux kept a copy of his script version of *Turnip's Blood*, and it is collected with her other papers at the Boston University library.

30. Whit Burnett was the co-editor, with Martha Foley, of *Story*, where *Turnip's Blood* was originally published; the magazine retained the copyright to the story.

31. Maddux found such collaboration—and the revisions of scripts required by producers—extremely frustrating. Accustomed to the burst of creativity with which she describes in *Communication* writing *Turnip's Blood*, the endless re-writing seemed to her arid and exhausting. In the notes written in 1968 to accompany the manuscript of *The Green Kingdom*, Maddux recalls the process of converting her story "Emmy Foster" into a screenplay titled "Love is Not Enough:"

> We did finish it and I enjoyed working with Lorraine and trying to learn to think visually (my writing had all been by sound up to this time, a voice heard in my head, as though dictating) but the continuous cycles of excitement, conferences, hope delayed, silences and final turndown I found very destructive. To be preoccupied over and over again with a story after the creative phase was over rendered me floundering helplessly. . . . (I once said to Sam Marx, "But people don't *have* alternate endings, and he said to me, "In Hollywood they do.")

Samuel Marx was the head of the Story Department at MGM.

32. The Record, November 1, 1946.
33. The Record, June 28, 1954.
34. Letter to Savington Crampton dated May 22, 1957.
35. Such record-keeping was important in Maddux's life as well. She referred to her journal as "The Record," and sometimes she returned to make additions to the entries of specific days when she remembered details she had omitted. This feeling that experience should be set down in writing emerges in her letters as well, sometimes in amusing ways. Writing to Savington Crampton about an occasion when Baker and a man he had met with were wearing identical ties, she reports asking Baker whether he had mentioned this when writing to the same friend, and being told that he had not. "That's the way it goes," Baker writes. "The important things are always being lost for lack of a writer's presence. I can't be everywhere." (Letter dated December 16, 1953.)
36. *The Green Kingdom* (New York: Simon and Schuster, 1957), p. 40.
37. *Abel's Daughter* (New York: Harper and Row, 1960), p. 161.
38. Letter to Savington Crampton dated August 11, 1957.
39. Letter to Savington Crampton dated June 16, 1958.

40.   Letter to Savington Crampton dated February 28, 1960.

41.   *The Orchard Children* (New York: Harper and Row, 1977), p. 8.

42.   Patricia Neal was very interested in playing Maddux's part in this drama, and wrote to both Maddux's editor at Harper and Row and Maddux herself. Neal was closer to Maddux's age, and so would have been more authentic in the role, but she lost out to the younger Shirley Jones.

43.   Letter to Savington Crampton dated February 28, 1960.

44.   *A Walk in the Spring Rain* (New York: Avon, 1978), p. 9.

45.   Letter to Savington Crampton dated January 24, 1944.

46.   Ingrid Bergman and Alan Burgess, *My Story* (New York: Delacorte, 1980), p. 427.

47.   *Fiction into Film* (Knoxville: Univ. of Tennessee Press, 1970), p. 141.

48.   Letter to Savington Crampton dated November 18, 1968.

49.   When Elmer Bernstein, who composed the musical score for the film, was told of Maddux's method of trying to convey musical concepts in words, he reported that he was not surprised, because the script had "emanations" that "felt musical" (*Fiction into Film*, p. 174.)

50.   *My Story*, p. 434

51.   Nashville *Tennessean*, October 28, 1979: 12-A.

52.   Letter to Savington Crampton dated June 3, 1979.

53.   "Thoughts from a Country Orchard," *Buffalo River Review*, May 18, 1983.

Rachel, about age six.

The "middle room" of Rachel Maddux's apartment at 16 West 43rd St. in Kansas City, Missouri, where she lived in the late 1930s and early 1940s and where she wrote *Turnip's Blood* and *Communication*.

Balcony of the apartment in Kansas City, with herb garden.

16 West 43rd St., Kansas City, with balcony at top right.

King Baker and
Rachel Maddux
in Chicago,
January 1942,
at the time
of their marriage.

Rachel Maddux and Savington Crampton in Washington, D.C., February 1943. Maddux's handwritten caption reads, "I smell the smoke, I taste the drink, I feel your arm. It is February 16, 1943. Rachel."

Rachel Maddux with her sister Erma (left), at Erma's home in California, early 1950s.

Rachel Maddux in Oxnard, California, in 1957, the year *The Green Kingdom* was published.

Rachel with one of her goats, Houston County, Tennessee, 1960s.

Ingrid Bergman with the goats used in the filming of *A Walk in the Spring Rain*, 1969. The photograph is inscribed "To Rachel Maddux—with much affection and gratitude for the lovely Walk in the Spring Rain—Ingrid Bergman." Photo by John Monte.

King Baker, Rachel Maddux, Margot Silliphant, Sterling Silliphant, Herb Wallerstein, Ingrid Bergman. Gatlinburg, Tennessee, April 1969, during the filming of *A Walk in the Spring Rain*. Photo by John Monte.

Communication

Being the Mental Autobiography
of a Sturdy Quest

by Rachel Maddux

Preface

It seems strange to think that I have waited a year to tell you these things, and then traveled two-thousand miles, allowing myself six days to accomplish the telling, and, in the end, to have returned without speaking because you would not allow yourself to hear.

I felt a great fear in you to hear, a refusal to accept what you thought would be a greater responsibility than you dared carry, a need to restrain me from a potential regret. Yet, by the last night, I almost wished to force you to hear, knowing that it is a far simpler thing than you think, knowing that I would never cast upon you more than you could wear with ease.

This is the story of a long and discouraging search for communication with a human being, for the recognition of someone else who was *attentive* to the same things *in the same way*, for another mind that could not fool itself. It has nothing to do with tastes in common. It was never concerned with agreement, easily found and of small importance, though pleasant.

These are the things I found in you three years ago and I recognized them instantly. That is why I said you were the end of the search. I did not mean there isn't another such person. I did not mean that this is all of life.

I only meant the search was ended because the
SEEKING
is done.

Now why should this be fearful? Why should you deny the validity of my find? What has this to do with age?

I had, that night, the steps of the search neatly in my mind so that they needed about fifteen minutes to make a straight line. But you said to write it. So now, without need for haste, why should I make a straight line? Why should I not meander? Why should I not take pleasure in the telling?

Of course I shall be prejudiced. It is my privilege to do myself justice. I am not compelled to tell you about the time I was so stupid as to try to steal a handful of sugar while standing in front of a mirror or about the time I hit Eloise Haycraft over the head with a doll buggy, or about my first infatuation at thirteen with a Swedish 'cello player named Ivan.

So I won't.

To
and for
Dear John

What I Thought It Would Be Like

As Elenor Murray would have been less clear without Barrett Boys, so I would now be only a third upon my way without my sister Erma.

She was the last new thing that ever happened to my father, the only thing he ever completely possessed that did not turn upon him or die or lose its savor. He used to tell again and again of how she would deny herself a trip to the circus in order to sit by him all day in silence while he fished; of how her obedience was so absolute that at his shouted command she stood still in the path of a runaway horse and missed being killed by an inch; and of how he once took her to the barber shop with him and stood her up in the window to be out of the way while he had his eyes closed. When he was ready to leave, there was a great crowd in front of the shop watching this life size "doll;" for Erma had taken him literally and, all the time, had not moved. When my father told that story he used to describe how my sister was dressed, the blue silk dress, the taffeta sash, the white ribbed stockings, and the velvet topped shoes.

Before my sister was born my father built an extra room for the house. Before my brother was born two years later, he built another one. Then he and my mother agreed that that was sufficient. But Erma wanted a sister and Victor wanted a brother, for which they used to pray every night and wish on every wish bone. And so, against the doctor's advice, my mother decided to try for a little brother. But Erma and my father had willed it to be a girl.

If God had only put my sister and my brother here out of curiosity to see how they would manage, he could have stopped

then. My sister got this wish without surprise and began succes-
sively on more difficult wishes. My brother did not and all his
wishes have dwindled. He is pleased now with an evening's enter-
tainment.

So I was thought of as Erma's child and I worshipped her from
the beginning and I do yet.

I told you that I very nearly died at first and was quite acciden-
tally rescued from being buried alive, but I did not tell you about a
little bulldog of a woman, a neighbor, who took an instant dislike
to my nurse. The neighbor brought her bed over with her and
stayed. One night about midnight she caught the nurse pouring
my medicine down the sink and refilling the bottles with water.
The nurse did not deny this at all but admitted very brazenly that
she had done it because if I lived after such an illness I would be
insane. My father cast the nurse out of the house in a snow storm,
not because of what she had done, but because she suggested that
a child of his could be insane.

Many years later, the daughter of the neighbor woman married
and was murdered by an insane man, the "snake killer" of California.

At three, when I recovered from the small pox, I became so
sturdy that it was thought safe to make up for my three years'
lack of discipline and, if not too late, to save my character. I then
suddenly became acquainted with authority. I did not understand
it, though I believed it. Finally I discovered that it was a kind of
medal for having stuck around longer than someone else and that
it was relative. My father could scold my mother but my mother
could not scold my father. However, she could scold my sister
who could not scold her but could my brother who etc. Alas, only
my teddy bear was younger than I and he was beloved. Why
should I scold him?

We were allowed to play only in our own yard and to walk on
the sidewalk as far north as the cottonwood tree, as far south as
Boston Avenue. A footstep on another's lawn was equally as bad
as rolling on it. The only explanation I could see for this was

relative age and its accompanying caprice authority. My sister never disobeyed this law, my brother often did, and so did I.

Grandmaw Brown, three doors to the north, a very lonely old lady of about ninety asked me into her house for candy. I stayed two hours. My mother was almost crazy, for there were gypsies in town, and when she found me she spanked me, explaining that the next time I was tempted I would then automatically remember the spanking and no longer be tempted. I waited until my father came home. Then I told him that I had been spanked because mother was older than I and she knew more than I did. He beamed upon me.

But Grandmaw Brown, I said, is older than mother, isn't she?

Yes, he said, she's ninety.

So she knows more than mother, I said, and she said I could go in her house.

After this I was never punished physically again and my mother, years later, actually apologized to me—not for having given me the wrong premise but for the spanking.

But what of the quest? What of the search? If authority was my first question, what then were the others?

I asked, why do you call only that a chair?

Because you sit in it.

What makes a train go?

It has an engine.

Why can't the cat talk?

Because it maiows.

It is true that you can sit in a chair (though once I called it a flower and sat in it to see if it would hold me up), that a train has an engine, that a cat does maiow; only for these answers I should have asked different questions.

During the war my crazy aunt came to stay with us for a time and while America gave up its sugar for the soldiers, we gave ours up so that my aunt could have it on her gravy. It seemed to me that she was very venerable, because the men who worked for my father would go to the store for their sugar allowance and bring half of it over to my aunt, because she had constant attention for every word she spoke, and because she got the answers she wanted. The war to me is always confused with my crazy aunt and with Peter Rabbit hiding from Farmer Brown, because as I told you Peter Rabbit was on the back of the paper and while my mother read it aloud we stared at the headlines on the front which had aroused such intense reaction in the skin of my mother's forehead a little while earlier.

I had affection and love but no communication and I soon discovered why. The great thing I lacked that other people had was a knowledge of reading. How simple. I would learn to read, then I would also know everything.

To this end I refused to show any interest in any other book except one called PETER AND POLLY on which I already had a head start. After several hundred readings of this aloud by my family, I had it memorized. I learned to count on buttons out of the button drawer while my mother sewed on the sewing machine. I then proceeded to teach myself to read. I would go through a newspaper tracing my finger on a line until I came to a word which I recognized. I would then begin the story of PETER AND POLLY and ultimately come to the word which might be the eighth word from the left, line 2, page 24 of PETER AND POLLY.

After a while I could recognize by sight any word that was in PETER AND POLLY. I began to ask what the gaps were one word at a time. It does not take very much to read a newspaper.

When I was five my mother began to undertake my education, so that I should be able to skip the first grade and thereby give credence to my father's belief that his were superior children. And so I discovered spelling. I was amazed; for I had thought that books had always existed and that all people had to teach themselves to read as I had. When I realized that some man had looked at those books a long time and had seen that the same letters were repeated over and over, that he had, in fact, discovered spelling, I was very disappointed that I had not discovered it for myself. It was a long time before I realized that one usually sees the letters first, that the letters might even have existed before the written word.

At any rate, I was now on the verge of achieving the necessary knowledge, so that people would allow me into the inner circle of direct contact. I had no idea of reading as a pleasure and no interest in fairy tales. To me it was something you had to do and get it over with, so that you would be allowed to do something else.

People, however, remained behind the glass wall; they had a film over their eyes. When I looked at them they looked over my head. So I concluded that I had been wrong and that the secret must be in the books themselves and to this end I read (still no truck with fantasy; I was sure that wouldn't get me anywhere). And, in a way, you do communicate with a book, you do focus your attention directly, you put everything else out of your mind. But the book cannot do it back.

And so I sought again and this time I knew I was right. It was exactly like authority, a simple matter of age and I concluded that it was only necessary to endure, to eat, to arise, to dress, to undress for sixteen more years. Then, when I was twenty-one, the world would open to me.

I would look at an oak tree then and it would slowly change from being a member of a group of trees to being this tree. It would shimmer all over and come to life, the way trees do in Walt Disney's cartoons, and it would show me its oakness and I would show it my rachelness. Also the grocery man would no longer be a list filler. I would look directly at him and he would not say anything silly.

He would say, I am Mr. Whitlock. There is a whitlockness about me that keeps me from being Mr. Moore. No doubt you see it.

And I would see it.

Wait then; it would happen. So I stopped seeking actively. This will be the time for drop the handkerchief. Now you sit in the classroom. Now you sing. Now you don't sing. When you are sad, cry. When you are pleased, laugh. Follow all the rules and it will make the years go quicker.

But you do not play drop the handkerchief alone, and so we come to

The Children

Oh, the sound of children's names! Of Marceille Drake and Ollun Ambrose. Blanche Pearce and Blanche Elgin and Maureen McKay. Of Booby Woolschleger and Sammy Martin and Kenneth Netherly. Of Eloise Haycraft and Zoa Margaret Graham and Grace Louise Laffoon. Of Mary Katherine Fox and Virginia Stephenson and Lillian Jensen and Eva Brownewell. Of Edwarda Misener and Mary Ellen Orebaugh and Frances Voorhees.

Of them all, Frances Voorhees is the only one who means to me now what she meant to me then; for I had the good fortune to lose her suddenly, irrevocably, to space instead of to time. Never, in all my life, have I been so defeated, so convinced of the individual's importance, as I was when Frances Voorhees' family moved to Salt Lake City. How bitter, how impossibly bitter, are the separations of childhood.

Frances Voorhees was different from the rest of us to begin with. We were mostly blonde with blue eyes; Frances had long black hair and large brown eyes. Her clothes were a little more sophisticated than ours, which is to say that they were simpler and sensible where ours were pretty. Also, her mother used to lie down in the daytime.

Then, too, there was her name, which gave me a great sense of satisfaction. Very early she explained to me that it was spelled es because she was a girl and, had she been a boy, it would have been spelled is. This seemed wonderfully logical to me. I was thrilled to think that thousands of people learned this fine distinction every year and didn't get mixed up on it. I was thrilled with the rightness that the long slender i was for boys and the round curved e for girls.

When I came to study geometry later, I had the same sense of satisfaction in the niceties of distinction, the rightness of logic.

If only I had read then what I have read now, I should not have been so surprised or shocked at the Voorhees' moving; for while in art there must be continuity and in life it is not necessarily so, still by coming to see it in art one is less shocked to find it in life. Perhaps it *is* always in life—only obscured.

At any rate, just as the shooting of the dog in OF MICE AND MEN is such a beautiful forecast of the shooting of Lenny, so was Mrs. Voorhees' attitude toward Frances' doll a forecast of her attitude toward their moving to Salt Lake City. Frances had a very beautiful doll and she wished to change the doll's name. Her mother would not let her change the doll's name. I did not see how she could do this. I did not understand what she was doing interfering with Frances' child. But most of all, I did not understand why Frances *accepted* it. She even tried to justify her mother's attitude to me. It was impossible for me to understand Frances' attitude. It seemed to me if she had changed her doll's name, she had already changed it. I did not see how her mother could tell her not to do something which she had already done in her MIND.

Much worse, I could not make Frances believe that she should rebel. I could not make her see the difference between what you do in your mind (which belongs only to YOU) and what you do with your hands (like breaking a dish or wearing unmated shoes). She put me in a very false and strange position. She made me feel as though I were looking at a very small mouse telling it, no mouse can be that small.

So when her family had to move to Salt Lake City I thought all the same things but I did not say them. I already knew I was beaten. I knew I was up against something too big for me and it infuriated me.

But what now of the other children and is it only because they did not move to Salt Lake City that I do not have anything left of them now? No.

It is because *even then* we did not have anything.

I got along with the children all right. I do not wish you to have the idea that I was in any way maladjusted or that I sat alone in a corner nursing my secret heart while they played games in the sunlight. They *all* played with me. They *all* liked me. Yet I was not more intimate with one than the others; that is to say no *one* of them sought me out for her special, for her best, friend.

This was because I was never angry as they understood it and because of something else which I will explain later. They were always in couples and always getting mad and making up. Each time that two of them would quarrel I would be very upset. To see them with their little hats and sweaty faces grimacing at each other, to see them shouting across the street at each other such terrible maledictions.

> You double dumb booby! I hate you! I will never speak to you again! I hope you croak!

I would be sick at heart. How terrible for them tomorrow, I would think. Here they can never speak to each other again and they have to sit in the same classroom together all year. How embarrassing!

But no. Tomorrow I would see them arm in arm *skipping* to school. It was incredible. I never understood it.

Only once was I angered at a playmate. Eloise Haycraft, to tease me in my passionate maternity, threatened to harm my teddy bear. She took him in his doll buggy and began to run over rough ground, round and round in a circle.

For a long time I did not even see her. I only saw that my baby's neck would soon be broken, that he would be knocked out of the carriage. I was a bad runner. I followed her around the circle many times, my eye on the teddy bear, great fear in my heart. Finally I saw Eloise in all this. I turned and ran in the opposite direction, met Eloise, took the teddy bear out of the buggy, set him on the ground at a safe distance, picked up the heavy baby buggy in my arms, raised it in the air and brought it down on Eloise's head.

I then picked up my child and walked home. I have just killed Eloise Haycraft, I said to my mother.

I never changed my feeling toward her. I suppose I hate her yet.

This not falling out and falling in the children did not understand and in a way they resented. Yet they used it to good advantage; for I carried all the messages of reconciliation between the ones who were not speaking.

The other thing, much more serious, which I said I would explain later was this: Sometimes one of them would come running toward me and about a foot from me suddenly stop. Mentally, they always did this. In anger with me or in exasperation, they never called down upon me their formulae of maledictions. They *all* always said the same thing:

You are old . . . old.

This is the first step then in one of the threads which runs consistently through the quest—this having been on a bad footing with TIME from the very first.

That same experience with children I have been through at least thirty times. It came to haunt me, maddeningly.

You are old . . . old.

Particularly since, being ahead of myself in school, I was always the youngest in the group.

Many years later I came to have my first real friend who *was* my special, my very own, friend but to this one, Aileen, belongs a chapter later on.

Perhaps it was because of this

You are old . . . old

that I came, much earlier than most people, to discover

Time

I had expected a great deal of my seventh birthday. Seven is a two year jump from five. Five is another world, the world of home. Six hardly counts. The five-year olds can belittle and disparage one year. Two years they accept and worship. At seven you are definitely of school. Nobody is going to drag you back. Nobody is going to be mistaken and think that you belong of home.

Quite early the day I was seven I was mildly disappointed. It was not enough different. The house should have looked different, the world should have given me a moment's attention.

Good morning, Rachel, the fence should have said, bowing low. Good morning seven.

There should have been fireworks.

I do not remember for sure but I believe it was not even Sunday.

Mildly disheartened, I went out into the backyard to be alone. I stood in the alley and looked up and down. I saw the neighbor's board fence. About eight inches from the top it had a horizontal ledge. I had somehow a great wave of tenderness for this ledge, for the feel of it, that it would hold a hand's grip. I became very sad. I forced myself to admit to the last dregs that seven was very little different from six—was essentially no different. I doubted if I had really changed any. I knew that the veil over everything was no nearer to being lifted. I had made no progress.

Suddenly, in a very sober moment, I knew, I knew all the way through me,

that eight would be no better than seven,

That nine would be no better than eight,

that ten—

that my parents, incredibly old as they were, were not so very different from me. They were not willfully withholding from me the secret of the maple tree. They did not know it. Mr. Whitlock was to them the grocery man—and nothing more.

I turned to look upon the world once more, to look with old old eyes upon the world and I saw the telephone pole.

The telephone pole was sitting in TIME.

I had been walking through space for seven years. The telephone pole and I would die and space would go on being there. But we would die BECAUSE Time went on being there. While I stood there, it was going on. Going on ahead of me, always ahead of me.

I was seven and time was seven and a half. I would be eight and time would be eight and three-quarters. I would have learned nothing, really nothing, and it would be over and time would be death and a half.

But this was not for me alone. My parents were going to die. From Harry to Zimmerly Streets were little houses. In the houses were people—all of them getting behind Time—all of them gradually dying.

Did they know it?

Surely not.

Of course not.

If they knew it they would not spend fifteen minutes talking about the price of eggs. They would not be so careless of one another. Why could not I climb up on the tower of the city hall and hold the minute hand still? Why could not I be crucified there, if need be, to hold it still for all the rest of them? Even if I could not stop the tremendous hand forever, I could at least hold it for one minute, one second, long enough for us all to catch our breath.

Would it do any good?

No.

The clock had nothing to do with it. While I hung there on the clock's hand, Time would go round and round the tower of the city hall, laughing. The clocks might all be wrong, in fact; too fast, too slow, ticking out last year's time, what did it matter to Time? Does the sea care if you spit in it? Does a storm have morals? Does the flood withhold itself from the cookie jar?

I stood in the alley and wept for mankind, wept for its minuteness, wept that the elements were unconcerned for it. I wept for the millions of people on the earth, for their smallness, for their fragility. I wept that they were all, all going to die and they could

Do Nothing About It.

And I wept that they did not know about it.

I wept that while they reached out their hands towards a tea cup, they were speeding the process. I wept that while I would be living the fullest, I would be dying the fastest. What they called death was nothing, hardly mattered. The dead people I had seen did not seem sad to me now. It is dying, slowly dying, all the time, every minute, WITHOUT ANY CHOICE that is so profoundly sad.

Also, it was unfair.

Also, it was infuriating.

And to think that I had felt impotent that I could not win against Mrs. Voorhees!

But what concerned me at the moment was that I could not explain this to my parents, that on this day my sadness would be interpreted as my not liking my birthday presents. I could see in advance that I would get into an impossible position explaining over and over that I liked my presents until, out of fatigue and the impossibility of being understood, I should cry and PROVE that I did not like my presents.

I washed my face and waited. They did not notice. I had discovered time and the only death that matters and it did not show.

Yet, strangely, humanly, I left my sister out of this. My sister was not pathetic, she was not fragile, she was not vulnerable, she was not behind time. She would never die. I also knew that she was not going to remain ignorant. I knew that she had begun to lift the veil and that she would someday know the answers. When she knew she would tell me.

Otherwise, there is a long gap in my memory about my sister. The last thing I can remember at this time is that one day in a great burst of spontaneity, I kissed her feet which were bare. She drew them back, jumped up and went into another room. I knew that I had embarrassed her but I did not know if it was because I had done it in front of my mother or because she felt that it was unladylike and immature to be caught barefooted. In my mind there is a great blank after this.

Of course it must have been at this time that I seemed very little to her (there is a difference of eight years between us). She was, I suppose, very much taken up with her own new world—

the world of the grown ups—and soon, too, she went away to school.

I have two very clear pictures however of the time before she went away to school. One was a night in which she read to me in her beautiful, low and rather husky voice

> Out of the hills of Habersham,
> Down the valleys of Hall,
> I hurry amain to reach the plain,
> Run the rapid and leap the fall,
> Split at the rock and together again,
> Accept my bed, or narrow or wide,
> And flee from folly on every side
> With a lover's pain to attain the plain
> > Far from the hills of Habersham
> > Far from the valleys of Hall.*

The other was a night she and her friend sat up very late making up a notebook for a Greek class in college. If she could find and assemble all those illustrations of statues I had never seen (statues she said were thousands of years old), if she could read that language which I not only had never seen but had never even heard of, then I knew that she would break through and would KNOW.

If there was more than one word to call a tree, there must somewhere be a word that had a treeness about it. And when she knew she would tell me.

Otherwise I remember mostly a continued process of self-imposed repression, lest in my great love I should again be so indelicate as to repeat in any form the kissing of the feet and so frighten her off.

But I would not have you think that I was completely without communication, completely shut off; for though I wore about me some invisible kind of hoop which kept off the children and while I feared to speak to my sister and while my knowledge of TIME

---

*Song of the Chattahochee—Sidney Lanier

made all adults so pathetic to me that I dared not try to penetrate their unrecognized tragedy, still I had

Tawm

Tawm lived in the rose bush.

Fabre writes of many experiments proving over and over the great ignorance of instinct outside its routine, the limitations of it. Just so is imagination surrounded with curious unexplained barriers. One experiment Fabre described was the changing of one condition in the wasp's accustomed procedure. The wasp would bring home its prey, carry it in the newly dug burrow, run outside, look around, return for inspection (?), and then exit and wall up the entrance very carefully. If Fabre robbed the burrow of its prey the wasp would return to the empty burrow for inspection (?) and exit to wall up the perfectly empty place just as carefully as though it had been full.

Here is a curious parallel. It seems impossible that an imagination that could create Tawm, could create him even to clothing, hair coloring, eyes, could make him talk, make him listen, make him play games—that an imagination capable of this could not make Tawm move.

Movement I could not manage. Tawm lived in the rosebush but he could not leave it. I had to go to him.

I spoke of Tawm exactly as I would of the next door neighbor boy. Exactly in this manner my mother accepted him. It is strange to think that she was able to show such rare wisdom and penetration all the way through concerning this imaginary child and almost none concerning my relations with other children. Much later I found out why. She herself had had an imaginary playmate and almost no real ones. Also my mother had, only a few years before, watched my brother play with such a boy as Tawm. My sister, she says, never had such a playmate.

Most children, I believe, have imaginary playmates and there are only two things unusual enough about this one to justify devoting so much space to him. One was that, though I have forgotten almost everything about him, this I remember: HE HAD NO AGE. Whatever it was that I was—he was my contemporary— exactly.

The other thing was that I killed him. He did not fade out of my mind slowly so that, in retrospect, I could not tell which day he was gone. He died one day and never came back.

Here begins then another of the threads—the destruction of whatever could have hidden from me my own loneliness. Sometimes you will see how I have deliberately chosen to destroy what would have lulled me from the battle, what would have blurred the edges of the search. Sometimes you will see how something in my own mind, despite my actions, has against my will killed my possible companions. Sometimes they died from causes with which I was not concerned, though I did choose them before they died. As this thread grows, though, you will see how it looks almost as though I had actually fought to preserve the things that shut me in from a small answer and made me seek on, bitterly, for a big one.

One day the rose bush caught on fire with Tawm in it. My mother found me screaming and thorn-scratched, fighting to save Tawm from the fire. She did not touch me. She said my name over many times. Finally I was quiet. There was no fire in the rosebush. Nor was there any Tawm there either. Nor would he ever come back. I was very lonely after Tawm was gone. My dolls seemed also less animated to me, though religiously I carried on the routine of caring for them.

As the golden fires of the golden age began to die down I began to wish for greater realism. Many times I heard of babies' dying. I did not see why the parents would not give me the dead baby (which they no longer wanted) to play with.

Several times I mentioned this wish and each time it occasioned great horror in the listener. Why did they always shush me so violently I wonder? Why did they leave me with the feeling that I with my golden curls and sweet blue eyes had said something horrifying? All that was needed was a little explanation on the processes of decay. Why did no one realize that I did not understand, did not even know about, decay? Or, if this was not what horrified them, why did they not explain to me that, even though they had put the baby in the ground, the parents were FAR from being through with it?

As you can see, this idea did not last long. I had, of course, much earlier discovered with a great sense of safety that no one can see into your head and that you can imagine what you please. So I began to imagine a baby of my own. Just as Tawm had his limitation of movement, so this baby had to abide by all the concepts of reality, even though it was always clear to me that it was only imaginary. This experience I have written of in MOTHER OF A CHILD, which you have already read.

Here again we see the thread which began with Tawm's murder. Though I had imagined carrying the child for nine months, though I imagined in my own way the labour and the delivery, something in my own mind would not let the child live once it was born. Something in my own mind killed this child too and would allow me no forgetfulness of the search for REAL communication.

How beautifully prophetic this thing was.

Tawm died in one day. The imaginary baby died in one second. I did not give up on my father so easily. I kept trying. I desired his attention so frantically that, the few times I received it directly (as when he sent me for something or when he tried to teach me something) I was so frantic with desire to please that I failed utterly and always brought forth the rage of his great impatience. Mostly, though, he was behind a newspaper or a magazine.

He had many years earlier tried to change his entire life in order to win my mother. He had tried to fit himself into the mold of the middle class where he did not belong and be a solid citizen, which he did not understand. At the same time he would have nothing to do with either one. Once he had been a great high hearted rounder, a beautiful dancer, a great drinker, a slender, nervous, laughing dandy of a man, living on his inheritance, having always a fine hound and a fast horse. His first wife dead, his inheritance gone, his child given to a cousin to bring up, he found himself burned out and tired at 25. He also, I think, felt just as unsafe and insecure as he had under the reign of his five stepmothers. Then he met my mother. He stopped drinking in one day. His last pair of dancing pumps wore out. He OWNED our house. Our horse, Dolly, was a family horse, a slow, safe mare. He held down for thirty years a very good but highly technical job of which he had no understanding but in which he was amazingly accurate by virtue of never failing to do all the things he had memorized from a little black book. Fearing being found out, he was automatically shut off from all communication with the people he worked with.

He paid cash for everything and he was profoundly afraid of dying and of starving.

Having made a change, he went the whole way in all outer things. He forced himself to wear clothes which made him look as much like a working man as possible. It is his shoes I remember best, high, laced, round-toed, and thick-soled—and his hat. But he was bored. He was profoundly bored. He had no amusements and no hobbies and no artistic accomplishments. He ate and slept and worked and read. He rarely talked. About every three months he had horrible, blind, incoherent rages followed by three days' silence.

And I would have died gladly for five minutes of his attention. To sit on his lap and be kissed I would have gone without food.

How then does such a forbidding person occasion such devotion in a child? Oh, I will tell you! There were the nights he felt good. They were rare but they were wonderful! Never was such a story teller. Never were such stories.

The little musk deer around whose tiny feet could be seen the rims of four dimes.

The times Mr. Baltimore lost all his diamonds on a bet.

The lady with a travelling theatrical company who stuck a hat pin in her husband's head during a performance and CONTINUED with the show.

Mr. Griffensteen's Indian wives.

My father's spitting tobacco juice in the cathedral.

My father's playing hookie from school to play casino with Maggie O'Rourke.

The fight my father and his father had over a goat, in which my grandfather lost the sight of one eye.

Shootings
    and
Saloons
    and
Wild Bill Hickock
    and
Fights
    and
Dances.

My father would always jump up and demonstrate the different kinds of dances—the buck and wing and the soft shoe dance and fast tap. This was my mother's signal to leave the room and to go to the kitchen and start making candy. She would start by making white divinity for my father and then, while she had her hand in, she would make a great plate of nut fudge and another kind with brown sugar.

And it would be long after midnight.

He was wild and glamorous and never satisfied with us. Children do not like comfort. They worship whoever demands the most of them. Therefore, I sought his attention. I did absurd, fantastic things. I memorized pages of a book on civil engineering in order to ask him questions, the answers to which I had just read. This got some results. When I saw it was in danger of becoming familiar I told him I would be an engineer. He told this to a friend of my sister who, being a reporter, put it in the newspaper. I was horrified to think that by having in print what I had said only to get my father's attention, I was then bound to go on with the lie forever. My father took my questions seriously and, one night, attempted to explain the workings of the transit to me (I was about seven or eight). I got so excited at all this attention that I would of course see nothing. He became so enraged with me that, after two hours, I still could not see the cross hair, that we never mentioned it again.

It was a year or so after this that I began to doubt the rightness of my father's ideas. I had already rebelled against the rages and, of the whole family, had refused to show that I could be upset by them, but the first real step came in the fourth grade.

My father insisted that we must excel all other children in school and I was able to do this in my own grade. He also demanded that we never admit to any ignorance, that if a teacher should ask us something we did not know we were to bluff our way through for the moment, go that night to an encyclopedia or some other source, learn the answer, engage the teacher in casual conversation the next day and introduce the subject to show that we now knew the answer for sure. For years he had us running all over town to find out what the teacher was paid to teach us.

One day I stood to answer a question. I knew only half the answer. I was planning to say the first half twice according to rule when suddenly I thought, My father is wrong about this.   I did not even answer the half I knew. I said in a clear loud voice, I don't know. The whole class, including the teacher, was shocked. That day I got more attention from the pupils than I had ever had. For days I would miss questions on tests on purpose in order to brag of my failures, so wonderful did I feel to be free of this unhealthy thing—his bluffing.

You would think now, a day that important in one's life, that I would be able to remember the question but I cannot, nor can I remember the half of the answer I already knew, nor the half I learned that day. But I remember the day. It was the first day I ever started to think on my own precepts by my own methods.

I was never free of my father's personality completely, nor do I ever want to be, particularly now that he is dead—but that day I was free of his mind.

So, that coupled with other considerations, it is not surprising that soon after this I became preoccupied with a desire for

Self-Sufficiency

So for a time I abandoned the search for communication in an extraordinary struggle for self-preservation.

I was about ten-years old and I came to be very concerned for my own sanity. Though I loved my sister I did not want to be like her. And I was desperately afraid of being like my father. Most of all, I wanted to be saved from my own sense of pity which would wash over me in such tremendous floods at times that I was frightened by it. I was frightened to the point where I was ready to put up a struggle against it. I saw myself becoming every day more and more like my sister and my father, yet I knew that they had some kind of safety valve which I did not have. They both had periods of tremendous gaiety, infectious, sweeping, hilarious gaiety. They also had periods of profound depression. My father would sit with his elbows on his knees, his head in his hands for hours, for days, once, a whole winter. Yet always there would come for them ultimately a time of fasting followed automatically by a time of sleep, followed by hunger and, once again, gaiety.

My depression was accompanied by violent headaches.

I did not believe that in me this cycle would always run its course. I was afraid that I would get caught in the middle of it somewhere and be stuck there. Then once I heard my father say proudly that he never had a headache in his life and this sobered me because I had been taking it for granted that his were the same as mine, only worse. I did not know if my sister had the headaches because, during the depression stage, she would hide herself away and afterwards, when she could be seen, I did not wish to remind her of the bad time.

Movies were terrible for me. They destroyed me utterly. I did not go to very many and the ones that got me the worst were the ones that were shown in the morning and had been chosen *for children*. One that knocked me out for days was called, I think, THE OLD WOODCUTTER. Another one was THE LAST OF THE MOHICANS. The stories in the newspapers were almost as bad. Once I read about an execution that was to take place at midnight. I lay in bed thinking now it is ten o'clock. He has two hours. Now it is 10:15. Now it is 10:30. By midnight I had a headache so violent I do not think I was quite sane. And one minute after midnight I tried and tried to realize as my own knowledge that a man was not in the world where, one minute before, he had been. I was ashamed of myself, that I had read about it and then just lain in bed, that I had LET that thing happen. I should have run to Topeka and clawed and scratched at the governor until he stopped it.

This feeling of responsibility held over me and later I actually did write a letter to the governor about a man who was to receive a long term for his fourth or fifth offence of stealing chickens to feed his motherless children. I got a letter from the governor and the man got pardoned, though I never knew him, and I was very much impressed by this, by what could be accomplished with the written word of a child when nobody will listen to the *spoken* word.

This writing, I thought, is a serious thing, not to be fooled around with. Perhaps that is where my respect for the written word comes from because, to this day, I cannot throw away a piece of correspondence and does the advertising firm for Voxy Vacuum Cleaners write a letter to me, I will read it clear through before I throw it away, and if they request an answer I am quite likely to carry the compulsion around on my conscience.

Yet while I was lying in bed suffering the condemned man's anticipation of being killed, I was in the background, quite aware of where and who I was, and I did not cry out because other people were sleeping and should not be disturbed except in serious PHYSICAL matters, such as an earache.

Though I did not realize the need at that time, how great was my pleasure long after to be in my own house alone. To be able to sit down, alone, with an idea, to know that I was doing nothing with my hands and yet I was busy, to know that no one around me was sleeping or getting dinner or waiting for me, that I could neither accuse myself of being lazy or depressed or sick, that I was simply sitting there in my own house, having an idea, having plenty of time to think with it just as far as I could get.

My father was inclined to be a hypochondriac and to accumulate a store of patent medicines. My mother thought this a great weakness, thought that her own strength was closely bound up with her country origins, with her having had to eat so much cornbread and to endure much because she had simply been isolated from quick help. She would not use toothpaste, I remember, but clung to the salt and soda she had always used and when the dentist complimented her on her marvelous teeth, she felt vindicated for all her ideas on health.

I do not know if she meant to give me the idea or not but at least I got it from her, the idea that there was something weak about poor health and something strong about hiding pain and not giving in to it. I got the idea that if you could hide it successfully you were saved from being ludicrous.

My father, by contrast, strengthened my mother's position because there was no denying that he was ludicrous about pain. When he was ill he would lie in bed with the shades pulled down and it was worth your life to go in that room or to speak to him. He would moan, loudly, though. He was just as upset about our illnesses as he was his own. At the slightest stomach upset, he would go pale and shake and call frantically for a doctor. He would sit by our beds, sure we were going to die, and the tears would roll down his face. Once when I had no more than a belly ache he sat by my bed, tears in his eyes, and said, My God, what have I done to deserve this?

Well, that really disgusted me because it was *I* who had the belly ache and so it looked as though my mother's attitude was right. So when I had a headache I would say I had a headache. She would say that she used to have them too when she was a girl. Well, I had said it once; I did not know how to say it more impressively unless I cried. This would put me in my father's class. She would tell me to go outdoors and lie down in the shade. I did not know how to tell her that there was a blinding light over everything and that I craved darkness. I did not know how to tell her that there were bells ringing in my head.

She had the country woman's distrust of medicines and fear of drugs. As she said, she did not like to take things. When I was older and discovered that by such a small thing as an aspirin tablet, I could dull those headaches I was mad all through to think how it had been withheld from me and I was madder to realize that some kind of fine distinction had been made between a tangible illness and an intangible one, that I had, in fact, been led into making this distinction myself. For if a child vomits, the greatest stranger will run to help it, but a headache is something different. It is not real. It has no cause. It has to be waited out. And its accompanying bells and lights, not being *real*, are some-how shameful and must be hidden.

So I would have to tackle them myself. In my mind they were associated with (and perhaps, I thought, caused by)

1. crying in the movies
2. feeling sorry for people
3. feeling affectionate and having no outlet for it, as to my father or my sister
4. getting excited
5. trying to explain something and not being able to.

I was sitting on the front steps grappling with the problem and I was going to get at the bottom of it. I was ten years old and it was early morning. Our house faced west and the house itself cast a cool shadow which reached almost to the sidewalk. Here the shadow made a sharp line. So must this day make a sharp line for me. No more must I go blundering about, crying and having headaches and reaching and not finding and leaving things unexplained. This day I must act. I must save myself from insanity while there was yet time. Nobody could do this for me. I and my insanity were all alone there together, face to face, in the shadow of the early morning and we were going to fight it out.

What was it now, exactly, when you came down to it—what was it that I had to conquer? It was the headaches and the need of people. What made the headaches?

Well—

Face it, now, what made the headaches?

Well, crying.

And what made the crying?

My emotions, I said.

Come on, now, don't lie. Say it all. Say it all, you coward. What makes the crying?

My emotions and . . . .

Go on! Go on! Say it all. Say it out loud.

My emotions and my fears.

Well, now, you have said it.

If you can say it, you can beat it.

The interesting thing here is that I said emotions *and* fears. Fear, to me, was not an emotion. It was a separate thing all by itself, deeper and more powerful than emotion. Also, you must note that while I did not realize it at the time, I left love out of this completely. I never thought of it. If I had, I would still have left it out, because this day I was concerned with detrimental, destroying forces. And had I thought of it, I would never have put love in this class. If I had thought about it, I would never have put it with the dark and hidden and secret things.

And you must remember that I was only ten years old.

I think now that this was quite an accomplishment for a ten-year-old but I did not think so that day. I thought I had only begun. I sat there on the steps with my knees apart, looking down at the step between my feet. Looking at the grain of the wood where the gray paint had worn off, I carefully sharpened the knife. I put it in and turned it around and around.

Come on now, your fears. *What* fears? What, exactly, are you afraid of?

Turn the knife. I am afraid of trains.

Turn it again. I am afraid to walk over sand or gravel on a sidewalk.

Turn it again.

Pause . . . .

And again, deeper.

I am afraid to say I have to go to the toilet in school.

That one was hard to say, wasn't it? I laughed at myself. I was brutal with myself.

Go on. What else?

I am afraid of my father.

You can't get away with that—you are a coward and a cheat. You can't be indefinite like that. *When* are you afraid of your father?

When his voice is loud.

You are lying, lying! If he sang loud, if he laughed loud, would you be afraid?

No.

Then *when* are you afraid of your father when his voice is loud?

When he swears.

Well now, you see, you can tell the truth if I torture you into it—if I am mean to you. What *else?*

I am afraid to meet or speak to anyone who is important or famous.

Why are you? Don't give me any lies now. *Why* are you?

Because they will know that I am *not* famous or important.

Well, it went on and on, a list as long as your arm and as I got older and learned more things to be afraid of I added to it.

I planned a method of attack and I began with the first one. I only had one method and I worked it on one of them at a time until I could pass a fear test and then I would cross that one off the list. This method was constant exposure. I went to the railroad track every day. I stood there gritting my teeth until the train had roared past. I did this every day for three weeks. I was no longer gritting my teeth. Then I took the test. I walked across the track in front of an approaching train. The train was at a safe distance— I was not interested in bravado. I *walked,* counting in rhythm, so that I would not run. I got clear across and proved to myself that I did not get my shoe caught in the track and remember too late to take out my foot and leave the shoe there. I did this three times. I went home and crossed the trains off my list and began on the sand.

After dusk I spread sand over the sidewalk. I walked, in the dark, back and forth, back and forth, on this sand, the noise tearing into my raw nerves. Night after night I did this until I found myself walking over the sand and thinking of SOMETHING ELSE. Then I crossed it off the list.

Going to the toilet in school, now, that was a little different. It called for a slight modification in the method. It called for a little further analysis; for it was not going to the toilet I was afraid of, or leaving the room, it was putting up my hand to ASK the teacher if I could go.

One day I just got up and left the classroom and did not put up my hand to ask. When I got back in the classroom I thought the teacher would scold me and make me stand in the hall. I was willing to pay in this way for the privilege of not putting up my hand. The teacher did not say anything. I began to have to go less often during classes.

My father's swearing also took a modification of technique. I went out into the back yard and whispered to myself Jesus Christ God damn hell. Nothing happened. I said it out loud. I said it quite loud. It was rather fun. It did not frighten me at all when I said it.

A great light burst on me. My father either did not know I was afraid of him, or at least, he was not *trying* to make me afraid of him. His swearing to HIM was like my swearing to ME. It was words, just words. If I could swear with my father's words, perhaps

I could think with my father's thoughts. I tried this. I pretended I was my father.

Right away I saw my mother through my father's eyes and I did not like to see my wife afraid of me. I sent my little girl to the barn for a hammer and I did not like it that she got so scared she could not even SEE the hammer. I did not like it but knowing it MADE ME WORSE, right away.

I was my father lying in bed, sick and moaning. Why was I moaning? I was moaning so that someone would come. Some one came. They came on tiptoe afraid that I would shout at them. Naturally I shouted. They tried to raise the window shade, raising it a little way and waiting for me to tell them not to. Naturally I told them not to.

This then would be the test.

The next time my father was sick and moaning I went directly into the room. I did not turn the door knob tentatively. I walked straight in. I did not tiptoe. I gave an imitation of being natural. I did not whisper or ask him if he were asleep as he was pretending to be. I did not try to raise the window shade or straighten the covers or walk aimlessly about the room. I sat down by him quietly and asked him where he hurt. He told me all about it.

Here was the secret then. If you acted as though he would shout at you he would not disappoint you. If you acted as though it were impossible for him to shout at you it would be. If you spoke to him seriously he would answer you seriously. Here burst another great light. My father was not only interested in what I thought of him, he was afraid of what I thought of him. He was afraid he would not be impressive enough. He was afraid of what everybody thought of him.

He was afraid that someone would think he was ignorant.

He was afraid my mother would laugh at him.

He was afraid to die.

My father was afraid. He did not know how to get over it and I DID.

Well, of course, I did not get it settled all at once. My father, through the years, would keep jumping on and off that list. The big thing is, that for every time he jumped ON, he jumped OFF again. In fact, towards the last he kept jumping off when he wasn't even on.

All these things took time, naturally. It was six years, working on it every day, before I really knew myself to be self-sufficient. I was sixteen before I got to the one about the famous people. The test for this one was a native girl, an opera singer named Kathleen Kersting, who had come back to the home town for a concert. I was to interview her for the high school paper and I did not know but what she was the very top grade opera singer in America. I hated doing it; for I thought she would be bored to death by this kid with the high school stuff. She was, however, very gracious, and this was such a shock to me that I wanted to explain it to everybody and so I wrote a very creditable story because I had something to say. I made myself take the story back to her, to the hotel where she was staying, and she was mightily pleased with it. I did not know how badly she needed publicity, even in a high school paper, and I am glad that I did not because then I would not have been able to cross this last thing off my list.

But you remember in the beginning there were *two* things: My fears *and* my emotions. For the emotions I also had only one method and that was, as they arose, to deny they were there, until they would cease to arise. How my mother must have suffered through this time, how she must have regretted giving birth to this hard, unlovely child, who would not let itself enjoy ANY-THING. How sad she must have been to find that in three tries she had not got one of her own kind, that in three tries my father's personality, his nervousness, had claimed them all.

I would go to the movie and sit there saying, I am feeling nothing; I am feeling nothing, until I had actually lost track of the plot. At first I would get seduced into feeling and then I would get up and go tramp around the lobby until I had swallowed the thing down. Then I would return and try again. Sometimes I had to leave four or five times during one show. Then I got so I could sit clear through a comedy. Then I got so I could sit clear through a tragedy. Then I got so I could laugh out loud when anybody else was crying. Then I got so the sorrow of the actors looked very ridiculous to me. Then I got so it looked neither sad nor funny to me. It looked like a fact. It looked like nothing at all. Year after year I would pay down my money to sit in a theater and exercise my freedom from emotion.

Once a friend of my mother's died. We were doing the dishes. She was washing; I was drying a glass. I said, That ought to help the unemployment. My mother looked at me. I looked right back at her. I could hear the noise of the tea towel against the glass, and I congratulated myself.

I saw a puppy run over and it did not touch me at all and I was proud.

Gradually I killed them all, the ones I had thought of and the ones I had not thought of and the ones I did not know about yet.

Besides my desire to save my own neck I had been influenced in all this by another fact. When I was about ten I became very disgusted with the fact that, upon going to the children's library, I would have all the books read on the way home and arrive at home with nothing to read. I was not at all critical of the contents of the books—just that they did not last long enough. My sister thought I was wasting my time with them anyhow and when I complained to her she let me use her adult card (against the rules) and took me down and showed me where the good stuff was. The good stuff was the Russians. It was Turgenev (by the radiator) and Chekhov and Dostoevski (by the window). It was in fine print and it lasted a long time. Also, a little later, I discovered Confucius (I do not remember how) and some very bad stories about Chinese people in a household magazine. Everything I read about Chinese was about the upper class Chinese. Everything I read about the Russians was about the lower and middle class Russians. I thought I was contrasting the Russians with the Chinese and I thought the Chinese had it all over the Russians. They did not go around making scenes and falling in fits and spilling food and soup over themselves. *They did not show what they felt.*

It only proved that I had been right to want self-sufficiency.

Well, I got it. After working on it for six years, I mastered it. It lasted for two years. I was afraid of nothing. I felt nothing.

I was very proud of it and, because I was not afraid of anything, I thought that the struggle had been courageous. From seventeen to nineteen I was in a most remarkable state. I slept only three or four hours every night and was never tired. It is not work which tires people; it is emotional battles and confusion. I was never confused.

My head was always clear. It was clear the second I woke up. Every day was just like walking on a tight rope. I had a job during this time (sometimes two or three in addition to going to school) in which there were five telephones on my desk which I had to answer in addition to doing a job not related to the telephones. I never got them mixed up. Without trying to, I had memorized some 500 telephone numbers just by hearing them once. Everything looked absolutely clear to me, as though it were made out of glass, and it was all perfectly static. It never moved.

I think I actually upset such a strong physical thing as the reflex arc. I insisted that *everything* must be submitted to my mind, that I should consciously control everything that had to do with me. By mistake I picked up a white hot crucible in a chemistry laboratory. Instead of dropping it, all this went through my mind:

You want to drop that crucible because it is hot. It represents six weeks' work. You would rather have a burned finger than to do that six weeks' work over again. Carry it over to the table and set it down *easily*.

I did this and I was proud of it.

I could do wonderful mental feats that I cannot do now, can never do again. I could memorize anything I chose to. I never wasted a moment and carried books around with me for all waiting times, for the street car, for drinking coffee, for the five minutes between classes. I sometimes read in this way twenty books a week.

But if you had come to me and said, I just killed my brother, frantic and shaken and almost out of your head, I would asked, Why? And I would have bullied you and browbeaten you and picked at you and made you go back and back and delve down and down until I had discovered why you killed your brother. And that would have been the end of it for me. An action had been done. I had found its cause.

So you see how it was that for almost six years I abandoned the search for communication. Sometimes I would think of it with nostalgia. I thought it was interesting. I thought it would be pleasant but it was a luxury. It was for those who had time for it, who were already safe. I did not have time for it. I jolly well had to save my own neck, my own sanity, while the saving was good. It would be nice to talk to someone, to be understood, to be HEARD, but I did not *have* to have it any more. I could get along without anything or anybody and I would be sane too.   Then when I had self-sufficiency, I was so proud of it that I forgot the search for awhile.

Several times I made little steps toward communication, though, little journeys away from the self-sufficiency and once I made a big step and that was

Aileen

I cannot begin to tell you how dull school was. I would sometimes get my lessons once and tear them up in order to do them over again. My sister had been pushed ahead so fast that she was almost a nervous wreck (but she made her goal; she was the youngest child ever to graduate from the Wichita High School with the highest grades. This was the goal she had set herself for my father). She made, however, a violent stand in my behalf. She declared I should not skip any grades, that it was a hardship to be always years younger than your associates and that they SHOULD NOT DO THIS TO ME.

My father took her word for it. The teachers would come and *ask* my mother to let me skip and my father would not let me do it. Erma had spoken. Well, my sister was right about that. It was not faster I needed to go, but wider.

My God, why didn't anybody tell me about non-fiction? I knew about text books and I knew about my father's engineering book but I thought they were to tell you how to do something. Why would you read a cook book if you weren't right away going to cook? I certainly never dreamed there were non-fiction books in the library with long time information in them. I certainly did think you would have to pay money for those books the way you did text books, that they wouldn't be bandied about *free* the way the fiction books were.

The way it was to me, you went to the library—you came out with a story book.

Well, was it my fault? Isn't that all they had out where you could see? Did they think a child could imagine a thing like a card catalogue by itself? Didn't those hidden stacks back there behind the desk look just exactly like the grocery shelves behind the counter where the customer MUST NOT GO lest he be accused of stealing? And wasn't the whole place wrapped up in SILENCE, in whispers, in mystery, and the goddamndest looking women in the world? And on top of that, weren't they likely any time to put me in jail for using my sister's card?

I went to the library. I came out with a story book.

You know what would have been just right for me? Inventions. I tell you if I had known that there were books describing inventions I would have gobbled them all down. Why the history of the Otis elevator would have been like music to me. And Fabre! *Think* what Fabre would have meant to me then. And a real, TRUE, account of an exploration !

To think I did not even know enough to ask for these things. All I knew was to ask somebody how a telephone worked and this is what I got. You speak on one end and it vibrates and it goes through a wire and it vibrates and the person on the other end puts his ear where it vibrates and he hears.

Well if you got answers like that and the books you knew about were story books and they wouldn't let you read your story books in school, what would you do? You'd wait, like I did, until you grew up and were rich. When you were rich you'd get you a telephone of your own and take it apart. You'd take one thing off at a time until it wouldn't work any more. The last think you took off, that would be it. You'd hold that in your hand.

Meanwhile, while I was waiting, school was very dull. I had no competition.

Enter Aileen. In the sixth grade. All is changed. She was five points ahead of me in everything. If I made ninety-five, she made a hundred. If I made a hundred she made a hundred and had neat penmanship to boot. Well, it got exciting.

She was also extraordinarily beautiful. And, in her way, she chose me.

How can I make you see her? She was so beautiful, so quiet, so calm, so utterly lovely. She was unhurried, always, and walked with a lovely, somehow mature, grace. In physical development she was ahead of all the rest of us; particularly I remember the calves of her legs were very shapely. She was very patient and unhurried and she never complained. It was a long time before I noticed that she never spoke unless she was spoken to. She never started anything, never volunteered enthusiasm, but whatever was asked of her she did to perfection and EFFORTLESSLY. She could not only get her lessons better than I could, she could do it in about half the time.

She was very beautiful. She had a large structured, strong, and peaceful face. Her eyes were violet and tremendous and she had a cleft chin. The thing everybody talked about, though, was her smile. It was slow coming and slow going, a constant flowing of the lips. Here's what that face was. It was mother. She was everybody's mother, pregnant and knowing a secret. That's what that smile was. It got everybody.

Then what a shock to notice how often the girl blushed. Blushed deep deep red clear to the roots of her hair. Everybody thought this was her purity and her goodness.

There is a kind of perfection which sets itself apart, beyond curiosity and beyond jealousy and beyond question. She had absolute, universal admiration. No one ever thought of being jealous of her. No one ever thought of questioning anything she did. Year after year in intermediate school she was always the president of everything. Isn't this remarkable? In the clubs, the girls would all say, There's no sense in having an election. Everybody wants Aileen again.

Aileen would sit there and blush, waves of red going over her face again and again. Everybody called this her modesty. I know now that she thought herself to be constantly overrated, living under some kind of false pretence, that she hated to have EVERY SINGLE mother in the school constantly holding her up as an example.

Well, she chose me, without being demonstrative about it and we wrote each other beautiful letters every day. How can I tell you of the wonderful hours I sat with her, being quiet, being happy, not talking, sitting there HAVING RESPECT FOR A HUMAN BEING.

We were in love with the same boy, who did not know it. Neither one of us went with the boys yet. One lovely day Aileen and I walked down by the river and sat in the sand. We wrote Clarence's name in the sand and beside it our names and we laughed to think how there was no jealousy between us, how it only proved how alike we were to choose the same one. We made up some very funny plans for sharing him, I remember. That was a happy day.

There was nothing about Clarence except his good nature and his blue eyes and perhaps he was older than the other boys. He grew up to be a fireman and I am sure that he is full of courage and full of good nature yet.

But there was something wrong. Here, at last, I had a friend and she never had any time. She always had to be going home. She rarely was allowed to go any place. She was always having to leave and go home early. If she had complained about it I would have been much quicker to catch on but she always acted as though going home was just what she wanted to do. And, as I say, nobody ever thought to question her or argue with her. It was unthinkable that such perfection would not be surrounded by perfection. She had a mother and a younger sister and a father. Her mother was younger than most of ours and her father was a lawyer. Professional men were very rare in the south end and we thought this added to the girl's good fortune. She had everything and everybody was glad that she did. In fact, this thing that I had been working on three or four years now, this self-sufficiency, that's what they gave her credit for. But she never had any time and at the last minute she could never go places where the rest of us were going.

Then I went into her home. She was supposed to go someplace with me and she was late and I went down to wait for her. She was doing the family ironing. None of the girls I knew were ever asked to do the family ironing. It was not so much that your mother thought it was too hard for you, she wouldn't trust you to do it *right*.

Aileen's mother was there. My presence did not bother her a bit. She did not say, Rachel is waiting for you. You go ahead. I'll do it. She let me wait it out.

I saw something evil that day, evil and incredible, and after I got away from it for awhile, I did not believe it. Here was this little skinny neurotic whining bitch of a mother, sitting around in her fragility (she was smaller than Aileen), gradually, maliciously, weaving a net around Aileen. I do not know yet how she did it, but she managed to blame Aileen for her ill health. She was making Aileen feel that she should get all the meals, do the washing, do the ironing, wait on her mother and her sister and her father, be there all the time, and still she could NEVER, NEVER do enough.

She was making that perfect child ATONE. I do not know for what. I don't think Aileen knew for what.

Later, as I saw that there was more and more of this, when I learned very tactfully that the girl had no spending money when her family was probably the best off financially in the neighborhood, I waded in. I wanted to fight this thing. I wanted to attack. To me it was the first out and out case of close to home injustice I had ever seen. I don't remember what I said but Aileen just looked at me. She blushed and said nothing and I shut up.

Another evening, when I had known her several years, she was at my house studying. I was feeling very enthusiastic and ambitious and I remember that I said to her, What are you going to be? And she said,

I don't know.

But aren't you ambitious? I asked. Surely you want to do something!

No, she said, no, nothing.

I was shocked. I just sat there being shocked. I was hitting so high with my brain. Surely with *her* brain, she must be hitting some really high mark. Dear God, here was my special, my best, my long awaited friend and I did not know the first thing about her. I did not have communication with adults and I had an explanation for it. I did not have communication with other children (you are old . . . old) and I had an explanation for it. Now I had a friend, my own age, my own size, and we did not know each other. Where is the explanation for that? Is it never possible then? I said. Are you always shut out? Are you always alone? Even friends—they do not speak honestly to each other?

Perhaps I had done well to want self-sufficiency. Perhaps I had better get back to work on it as fast as possible.

Not only was the girl allowed no spending money (to which she would not admit) but she was not allowed to have the very simple, innocent attention from boys that we were all allowed. She was not allowed to have a boy carry her books home from school even.

Then Aileen did a curious thing. She began a friendship with the school tomboy. This girl, Brownie, was a little stocky bulldog. She was wonderfully good natured and the star athlete and a terrible student. Everyone naturally thought that Aileen was trying to reform her and watched with much interest.

Nobody knew, except me, that it was Aileen and not Brownie that was getting the benefits. Well, it was the sweetest and the most innocently beautiful courtship you ever saw. The two of them were so beautifully happy and they went around glowing and everybody thought it was lovely. I was so glad to see Aileen radiant that I was not even jealous. Brownie would go around saying to everybody, Isn't she beautiful? Isn't she wonderful? And everyone would laugh because Brownie was so cute about it. Aileen had a beautiful voice and people were always asking her to sing. She would go and ask Brownie what she should sing and Brownie would tell her and then she would stand up on a stage or a little platform or the front of a classroom in her perfect, lovely poise and her eyes would hunt until she found Brownie and then she would sing just for Brownie, the corniest Irish ballads in the world. We would all look at Brownie and Brownie would blush and we would all be tickled to death to have touched such sweetness. And suddenly it was fine and everybody was glad that Aileen got to go places. I was glad that Aileen must at last have put up a fight against her mother to get some free time, but now as I look back on it I think Brownie's having money must have had a lot to do with it. Now that I look back on it I think Aileen's mother must have been very ambitious and must have hated living in that part of town, which was not fashionable and she must have held them all responsible. And Brownie would bring Aileen presents. Here was this poor student, this little bulldog of an athlete, able to see what none of us had seen. Brownie had sense enough to bring her presents. Why had none of us thought of it? Why, because you never think of the queen as needing anything you've got. It took Brownie to find out that the girl could be thrilled to actual tears by being given an eversharp pencil or a bottle of perfume or a little trick comb or a compact. We had never noticed she didn't have these things. And Aileen was not trying to reform Brownie as they all thought. She was not trying to make a good student out of her. She did not bother Brownie with her lessons. She simply sat down in the evenings and did her homework for her while Brownie would practice a new basketball shot.

Well, we all graduated from intermediate school and Aileen had the top honors and I had the next to the top and then we started to high school. And Aileen had all the honors and nobody could touch her. She stuffed Brownie down everybody's throat and everybody took it. There was no touching the girl. She could do no wrong and she was the president of everything again and in her first year too.

That summer just before we started back to the second year of high school we all went to camp. This was a YWCA camp and Aileen had to be there for the ceremonies that we had that night but her family would not let her stay at the camp.

The ceremonies were very impressive and very sad. We all had little lighted candles stuck on pieces of wood and vowed something or other there in the dark, in chorus, and then we went down to the river and set the candles afloat. You could see them for a long time floating down the river in a single line and finally they all went out and we turned from the river and walked back in the dark to the camp and then Aileen had to leave us and go home.

She not only had to leave us when we were all so jolly and cozy and full of being together in the dark after the lighted candles, she had to go home to an empty house; for her parents were out somewhere.

She got her father's gun

and

she blew her brains out.

Just one shot, you understand, aimed to kill instantly, without even disarranging her face. This from a girl seventeen years old, who had probably never shot a gun in her life. She always did everything perfectly. She left no note.

And I, who always picked at everything until I got to the bottom of it, I thought the greatest compliment I could pay her was to leave it unsolved. I said then, I say now, I simply do not know why she did it. I leave it at that.

But others didn't. Next morning all hell broke loose. There was a very sensational newspaper in town run by three brothers who had been run out of every town in America of any size. They knew no better. I still do not know how it was they weren't sued for libel. They did not hint. They simply blasted. Here were the strange words, then, words the people of Wichita had never heard before. There was the word homosexuality.

There was also Lillian Jensen. She was the daughter of a very common woman and a fine, silent sailor father. She had been brought up on a steady diet of chili and The Chicago Herald & Examiner. On Sundays she used to go to church and hear the Bible read, come home and read the Chicago Herald & Examiner, and eat a chicken dinner, all with the same gusto. This girl had a snapshot of Aileen and Brownie. Brownie had on overalls. Naturally she did. She had that day mowed the lawn and cleaned out the furnace. The reporters got hold of Lillian and put words in her mouth. She was thrilled to death to be so important in a case equally as good as any in the Chicago Herald & Examiner.

The whole town was in arms. It was like the descriptions you have read of the hours before a lynching. The yells of newsboys were every place. Every one went crazy. No one had any knowledge. High School and college teachers asked me questions which plainly showed that they did not know the difference between a homosexual and a hermaphrodite.

The town's theory was that Brownie was an hermaphrodite and that she had raped Aileen and got her pregnant. Christ, isn't that fantastic? And *thousands* of people believed it. On the streets, in street cars, perfect strangers would stop me and ask me the most horribly fantastic questions.

And I swear to you that I had to explain to Brownie what they were accusing her of! She didn't know!

While I was explaining to her (for I stayed with her all those first mad days) I thought how is it I know this? No one ever told me. Then I knew. Years before a true lesbian had moved into the neighborhood. She was only a child and we had played together. I liked her very much and it seemed perfectly natural to me that she was the way she was, that she was ashamed to have lace on her petticoats, that she rode a bicycle so beautifully and so easily, that she ran a spike through her leg and sat there swearing and swearing and *pulled it out* without crying. I had known her for years. Everything she did and said seemed very logical FOR HER and I had simply accepted it.

While I was explaining to Brownie, I realized that a child ON ITS OWN OBSERVATION *never* makes a moral judgment. All condemnation, all persecution on moral grounds, is acquired.

You see, Aileen was the perfect child. She could do no wrong. The people of the town were sure wrong had been done, horrible wrong had been done; therefore they must persecute Brownie. Leading the pack was Aileen's father, the lawyer. He was going to have the girl put in prison and they dragged her through hell before she got out of it.

This was the time when I realized that because something is printed it is not necessarily true. I have never trusted either newspapers or gossip since.

With Aileen dead it left me in top place. Right away I learned how hollow is honor. Some I refused to take.

But of all the people to defend Brownie, I was the logical one. Not everyone could have got away with it and I was trading on my family and highly on my sister's reputation in this same high school. I took Brownie back to school. Now I don't know why I thought it was so important. Everyone thought she would change her name and leave town. I bullied her into going back to school. She wanted to go out to Aileen's grave (she had been barred from the funeral) and kill herself and now I wish I had let her. But I stood over her like a hawk and I took her back to school. There was a mob in front of the school. There must have been 2,000 students there. We had to walk down a sidewalk a block long. I told her to look at the tower and not take her eyes off it. I looked at the tower too. We walked slowly straight ahead, looking to neither side. They simply fell back and made a path for us. There was almost complete silence. I took her in and locked her in the toilet. Then I went and fought it out with the dean of women. For several days I went to all her classes with her. I owned the world in those days. I knew no fear. I would have as soon as not fought the whole school.

I doubt if I could do it now.

My parents showed wonderful sense through all this. My mother, mainly, because she did not understand what it was all about and my father because he had known Brownie's mother when she was a girl, and because he always defended whatever was being attacked and because I am sure he thought I did not know what I was doing. They simply left me alone.

To take a stand like that—naturally it brought repercussions. Such a spectacular defense, well it brought them all out from under cover. Strangers would come to me and say, I have been hiding all these years; I have been afraid. I have no one to talk to. Surely you, who are so tolerant, will listen to me. I listened, I listened to them all.

I sought communication, I thought, *I* who have a right to speak to anyone. Even if I cannot find it for myself, at least I can GIVE it to these, who have not the right to speak to anybody.

There was another thing which encouraged me. The ones in high school were the ones who had been shunned by playmates, had been excluded, and had therefore been driven back on books. They were the only people in high school, except Hugh (whom I did not discover until later), who had read the books I had. Therefore, in my mind, homosexuality was a sure sign of superior intelligence. It was a long time before I discovered what dilettantes most of them are, how they simply crawl around on the edge with their small appetites and their small talents and rarely tackle a big thing, how they are always cluttering up the periphery of what is creative, but they rarely create.

But I did not know this then. I listened and listened and listened. At first I would very tactfully question, keeping a certain amount of delicacy, but it was unnecessary. They were dying to tell ALL. How when they were little they had known there was something wrong, but how each one had felt himself to be alone in the world like this. And then the joy of finding others like themselves.

Well, I was interested. I was curious. I was learning every day. It was flattering to be the courageous defender of justice, it was flattering to be so useful to so many people, to be sought out for advice, for HELP. Oh, I longed to help.

It was not long before I knew all the homosexuals in high school, real and converted. It was not long before I knew all the ones in town (and that was a goodly number). Pretty soon I knew the alcoholics and the marijuana peddlers and addicts and the crazy people and the neurotics.

And then, I realized, that with but a few exceptions, that was ALL I knew. They had all my time. I could not go in any restaurant in town for a cup of coffee and sit down and drink it ALONE.

But I had fifty beautiful complete case histories all written out.

Well, you can see how the high school classes didn't interest me much. I learned two things in high school. I learned that literature is not dead and I learned how to rebel, and neither of these, needless to say, from the teachers.

I met Hugh and Hugh knew that literature is not dead. We were such good friends and he knew such wonderful things. He knew about the New York Times, for example. Now I would never have thought of living in Wichita and reading The New York Times. But he did. And there was intimate gossip about the writers of books coming out JUST THAT WEEK. And it looked as though a whole lot of people were concerned with these new books, that they were just waiting for them to be out so they could read them.

Hugh knew what was on Broadway that very night.

He knew about Sherwood Anderson and WINESBURG, OHIO. I cannot begin to tell you what that book meant to me, those stories about people JUST LIKE THE ONES I KNEW, those very simple stories, where the words coming out of people's mouths sounded just like the words coming out of people's mouths—not going through the author's head first.

Hugh knew about the New Yorker Magazine.

He knew about literature and he taught me, without ever saying so, that it can change and be new all the time, that it is very much a part of daily life, and that the plot is NOT the thing.

He was the most important thing in high school. He was my friend. He was well dressed and gay and handsome and always enthusiastic about some new thing and you could go any place with him, sit up half the night drinking coffee, and talk, talk, talk, and he never touched you.

The others were always jumping at you and grabbing you and hating you, sometimes hitting you, for being cold, for being cruel. It was all very bewildering.

Yet after we were in college, I found that with Hugh you *had* to talk about books and Broadway and literary gossip and nothing else. You could not talk about yourself. That bothered him. You certainly could not talk about *him*. That scared him. You had to keep it impersonal and safe, or he would run off and leave you. He could never stand any kind of human trouble or if we were anyplace where there was a scene, he would simply disappear. There came to be, for me, a time when I thought that if two people are talking to each other they should have something more important to say to each other than the lives and writings of OTHER people. But that was much later. In high school Hugh was just right. He was wonderful for me and he gave me the idea that there were probably just thousands of people in the world I could talk with if I could just find them. I got the idea that there would be just LOTS of them in New York City, for example, and it comforted me, because I didn't think I had so very long to wait.

The other thing I learned in high school was how to rebel. I resented bitterly the constant all pervading authority in high school. It has changed a great deal since my day. For a long time I just hated, hated, hated it, having to account, having to explain, never being trusted to do the simplest thing without supervision. We were not even allowed to have school dances.

My first class every morning was out in an annex and I could not make it on time to my second hour class without running up three flights of stairs. This was gradually becoming difficult to do, because of a back injury I had had many years before.

It was a quite severe injury and, at the time, my mother had taken me to a chiropractor, knowing no better. The chiropractor was a woman who worked in her husband's furniture store and had chiropractic as a kind of hobby I think. She weighed about 200 pounds. She laid me down on a table with a support under my chest and one under my knees, then she applied her 200 pounds and let her feet off the ground. The back got much worse and I knew that this was wrong. I told my mother I did not want to go back. She thought since it hurt so bad that it must be doing a great deal of good. She also thought I was trying to avoid pain, the way a child will swear it does not have a toothache when you get it down to the dentist's office. After several times of this I found that the only way I could keep from having my back broken completely without being accused of being a coward was to tell her it was better. I did. We forgot about it for awhile. In high school, under the gymnasium work, it got very painful and we had another little flurry of treatment. We went a step up this time. We went to an osteopath. The osteopath was very subtle. He just rubbed my back and put me to sleep. Naturally I felt better. That's why they do it in hospitals. You always feel better. Only my back hurt. The osteopath himself saved me this time from any further damage. He did not find much wrong with my back but he discovered some kind of obscure female difficulty, which scared my mother to death and which she dismissed as nonsense and he wanted her to pay *in advance* for some twenty or thirty treatments. Anyhow, it was a matter of laying down a couple of hundred dollars and my mother's native good sense came to the fore and she knew there was something that smelled, so she refused.

So we just dropped the whole thing. My mother herself had always had backaches and she considered whatever she had to be perfectly normal. She also considered them to be the logical accompaniment to adolescence, and if that is true, I had the longest adolescence you ever heard of.

Well, you get used to a thing, you know. It only changed the tiniest bit every day, and automatically you adjust your life to it. Automatically I began to do everything sitting down; I began to be careful not to drop things so I wouldn't have to bend over to pick them up; I taught swimming (which I could do) in exchange for getting out of tennis (which was a nightmare).

And my mind was working at such a fast clip that I didn't have time to think about it. But those three flights of stairs every morning got more and more difficult. One morning I was trying to run up them, hating, hating, hating, doing it and I stopped. Why was I running? I was running so that I wouldn't be late. Was I afraid of being late? Is that a crime? No. I was afraid of the teacher. Here I was almost out of high school and I had exactly the same conception of a teacher that I had had in the first grade. But that was ridiculous because I was really not afraid of the teacher. I was just carrying over old habits. After all, what would they do to me if I was late? They would make me stay in an hour after school. Well, what of it? Was it worth it for the privilege of walking up the stairs slowly? Yes. It was worth it. I walked.

The teacher naturally supposed I had a good excuse and asked me why I was late and I caught myself starting to tell her about my back. So there was my moral victory of the stairway. She was giving me a chance to slide out and I was going to have my cake and eat it too. I was going to disobey a rule and then slide out of the punishment on a physical excuse.

I'm just late, I said.

The teacher had known my family and she had either known

or heard about my sister. She didn't want to turn me in. She stood there and gave me every possible chance to lie out of it. Was your first class kept over late? Were you sick? She was giving me every possible chance, but I was holding my new found freedom to heart. I was just late, I said.

She thought I did not understand the punishment and patiently explained it to me. I said I didn't mind it. Reluctantly she turned me in.

Almost every evening I stayed an hour after school. I read a novel each day. I never resented the punishment. It was getting simpler to me. When you are up against authority find out what the punishment is. Weigh the punishment against what you want to do. If it's worth it, go ahead, but then you must never try to get out of the punishment and you must never resent it.

It was a great thrill, somehow, each night to be coming out of a building (which is habitually full) when it is almost empty, and to be coming out into a deserted quiet because you have made your stand against authority and paid for it without quibbling. You get to prove each evening that you can think for yourself and that you as an individual are not afraid of an established authority.

It has always been a very thrilling moment to me since to be working on a night shift and leave a place that is in the usual hours humming with activity, to leave it when it is quiet and almost deserted, and to go out onto the deserted streets which were, a few hours ago, so full. I suppose that is why I like to work nights or to come out of a theater behind the crowd or to be any place where the crowd has been and is no longer. I always feel as though I had just gained my strength by winning a moral victory.

It was all, you see, a part of the self-sufficiency upon which I had gone back to work in earnest after Aileen died. Well, I had crossed the last thing off my list. I was sure I was not afraid of anything. I was self-sufficient and I was just as proud of it as I could be. The summer after I graduated from high school, I went to work in an office and it was here, when I was least looking for it, that I discovered that self-sufficiency is not a great, free, sunlit meadow as I had thought. It is a deep well with a high wall around it and I wanted. . .

Out

I was working and I was earning my own money (not much. I worked nine hours a day and a half day on holidays for $6.00 a week, then $8.00, then $10.00, then $12.00) and it was a good feeling. I was always busy and I was never idle and I was perfectly content.

There were two very stupid girls in this office who were employed to fold circulars, being incapable of anything else. They would get so bored with the endless folding that they would go to the restroom and just stand. They did not smoke and were simply standing there in order not to be working. The plumbing was defective and there was always a fluid layer of filth about a half-inch deep on the floor. They did not seem to mind this. There was a large mirror in the room and these two girls would stand staring, each at her own image, and carry on an endless conversation. It went like this:

Whaja do last night, kid?

We went to the movies, kid.

Whaja see, kid?

The Palace, kid.

Was it any good, kid?

Day after day the same except for the various descriptions of physical ailments, kid, and what the doctor said, kid, and you ought to try this, kid.

One day in the noon hour we were all in the restroom having a last cigarette before starting to work. The two stupids were staring into the mirror as usual talking to their own images. One had been absent the day before.

Didja miss me, kid?

When, kid?

Why, yesterday. I was sick, kid.

Was you, kid?

Yeah, didn't you even miss me, kid?

Naw.

Whassa matter? Don't you love me no more, kid? The other one turned on her.

No, she said, I don't love you. She raised her eyes and took in all our images in the mirror. I don't love any of you, she said. She stretched her arms above her head. I don't love anybody but my Howard, she said, and I love him like *nothin' human*.

Then she turned and, chin up, walked gracefully over the filthy floor, like a queen, and I want you to know that they were all quiet and they were all impressed and they made a path for her.

The earth began to quake for me and the far off thunder to sound and a chasm to split and yawn before my feet. Here was this stupid little moron with her blank doll's face set atop her scrawny body waking me up with words from her weak cupid's bow mouth.

The way she felt about Howard. There was not a man anywhere about whom I felt like that. This stupid little creature had fast in her hands something *I* could not even touch.

Without meaning to I had killed this capacity along with the fears and the pity. It is all of a piece. If you want one you have to take them all. I realized suddenly that while I was never depressed any more, neither was I ever hilarious. I tried to think back to when I had laughed last. It had, of course, not been since I had cried last. You cannot go any higher up than you can go low down. It was a sad and defeating fact. Ecstasy may not be for the strong, I thought, but I would rather have it.

Well, I had wanted to be self-sufficient and I had over done it. I had made a mistake, that's all, and it was lucky for me that I had found it out in time to undo it. I was going right out and begin to feel things again. But it was not so easy. You get to fooling around with the emotions you were born with and you get something started which will generate its own power. It is like an accumulative poison. I had never meant things to go so far. I only meant to roll the snowball half way down the hill. Right away I was going out and feel things—and nothing happened. Nothing. I would expose myself to pitiful situations and feel no pity. I would go to the movies and say, Now I am feeling. This is sad. This is very sad. And there were no tears. I would throw myself into what I hoped would be a love affair. I would go through all the actions, waiting to feel something, waiting, waiting. I felt nothing.

Horrible things happened to me. The more I tried to change the worse I got. This coldness, I know now, gave an impression of great tranquility and it attracted people to me, particularly men who thought I was much older than I was. Each one would come up against that coldness and be delighted because he was absolutely sure that he was just the very guy to break it down. Then he would come up against it again and again and finally, in frustration, he would want to force me to feel something—even anger.

I was kidnapped three times and I had my head hit with the butt of a gun and I had it banged on a car door handle and once I was strangled on a road and thrown into a ditch which, fortunately, was full of cold water, and several times I was beaten up. One very fine and brilliant man became so utterly confused that he tried to kill us both in a car and later tried to kill himself. And I was always completely relaxed and silent and never frightened and each time I thought I would be killed and I did not really mind.

It was all a great puzzle to me. I had not the faintest idea what was going on in these people. I had no idea what made them act the way they did. I thought it was just a coincidence that I kept meeting crazy people.

I never told my family of these things because I knew my father and my brother would simply go out and kill the man and I did not want my father to hang for something which I felt must, in some way, be my fault because it happened so many times. But I can tell you I was fed up with being knocked around and I was bewildered by having aroused such universal hatred in very simple people and I was very very discouraged over ever being able to feel anything.

I sat down and had a session with myself. You made a mistake, child, I said. You made a serious mistake. It took you seven years to get in this state. It is quite likely it will take you seven years to get out of it. Even so, you will still be young. You had better not go out with people for awhile because one of them is likely not to be so impressed with your lack of fear and he will be able to get you killed clear dead. The thing to do is to accept it and quit trying. Study your lessons and wait awhile. Ignore it. Maybe it will work itself out.

So I studied my lessons and I read philosophy and I began to think again about ideas. I cannot tell you how thrilled I was by the evidence of evolution. It is so different from knowing the general theory—so different to be able to reconstruct the world from a little cell that you have SEEN, to add stratum upon stratum of complexity, tying it always to the stratum below. Oh, it was wonderful!

I worked out a philosophy of my own called The Theory of Fundamental Rhythm. It was very scholarly and I worked on it for months. It was a great thrill to sit in a strange room looking at a door divided into two panels, to divide it, mentally, into four, eight, sixteen, thirty-two, sixty-four. To split it into molecules of cellulose, to split the molecules into atoms and the atoms into protons and electrons and those into positive and negative charges of electricity capable of being wood, not because of the *number* of electrons revolving around a proton, but because of the *rate* at which they were revolving. To be able to do this (with variations) to sensations and perceptions and memory and ideas and to have them all in their complex and various rhythms resolve themselves in the aggregate into one very simple fundamental rhythm (like a great heart beating) which could generate new beginnings, the way that a waltz and a foxtrot and a march all will when played simultaneously.

There was a great deal more to it than this, but this will give you an idea (of course I thought it was NEW) and it was a wonderful thing to carry around. I could sit down anywhere and, without speaking a word, start it off running in wave upon wave through my mind.

It was so clear in my head I wanted to explain it to everybody. I did not want them to wait another day without knowing this wonderful thing I had discovered.

It had a very serious hole in its logic which I did not discover until later, but even if it had not, it would have died on me later, because that is the fate of all far reaching explanations. In their immensity, they carry the seeds of their own death. It is not in its simplicity that the world is rare and wonderful and ever interesting; it is in its infinite complexity. It is not by being a piece of the universe that a man achieves his immortality in your mind; it is just by the very things which make him stick up like a sore thumb.

There is a time in our life when you need to see the world as if from a star, when you need to believe that it is logical and ordered. But, later, there is a time for coming down from stars and seeing it as a human being and the thing that makes a human being human or a spider being spider is not a general impression; it is a multitude of details, illogical and unordered and wonderful and rare and never never explained.

But not for now. Now we are looking from a star and The Theory of Fundamental Rhythm was the greatest thing going and my sister came home.

She had been away a long time, had been living in the Virgin Islands. She had a husband and a baby and she discovered me. All these years I had held onto her as the one perfect being I had ever known, but she had been writing me the sweet and gentle letters that you write to a younger sister and recommending to me books which I had read long before. But she was never set in her ideas and she changed her mind very fast. We were friends. It was not just the accident of being sisters. We had discovered each other.

It was truly wonderful what she did for me.   She would *sit down* and we would talk. We would go down to Collins Cigar Store, just the two of us, and sit there in the back booth smoking cigarettes and drinking coffee and she did not make me feel that she was just killing time until she could be with her husband. She made me feel that I had a perfect right to claim her time. She made me feel that she was really excited to be with me, that the things I had to say were just the things she wanted to hear.

It was the nearest to communication I had ever been. I told her about The Theory of Fundamental Rhythm and she was actually convinced of it. She asked questions and I explained it to her and she was really thrilled by it. Nobody else had been. And this, I want you to know, about a subject and a way of thinking that was absolutely foreign to her. Analysis and dissection were never her way, but she was perfectly willing to believe that they were MY way. All scientific things and their methods were to her akin to all mechanical things, which were without soul. Put her face to face with the simplest mechanical contrivance in those days and she would immediately instill it with a hostile personality.

But she was not trying to convince me of her way. She was listening to mine. And I can tell you I needed a listener the worst way. The first thing I noticed was that she asked questions. I had tried to stuff this theory down several throats and, while others would appear to be listening and they would say it was interesting, my sister by contrast was actually trying to avail herself of it.

Many, many other things she did for me too.

She had, among hundreds, two very rare qualities. One was that she took it for granted that you were responsible, were, in fact, an authority for your own statements. To your statements she only applied your interpretations. Her own interpretations she applied to her own statements.

The other quality was that each day died at sunset. She never reminded you today of what you had said yesterday. This is the thing that mothers can never manage. (And I often wonder if she herself will be able to do for Robin, her own son, what she did so brilliantly for me). Mothers are always reminding you this week of what you said last week; for they have forgotten that to a child the weeks are sometimes worlds apart and last week seems very childish to you this week and you would rather not be reminded of it. Mothers are always reminding you when you are in the midst of a beautiful friendship with Beth, of your recent and disastrous friendship with Mary. My sister never made the mistake of thinking that any two friendships could ever be alike.

Upon the subjects which were yours she gave you the impression that she did not do any thinking on her own. She had very little of what is called curiosity and you could tell her 5/16ths of a thing and be perfectly sure that it would remain 5/16ths. She would leave it wherever you left it; she would never sit down by herself and manufacture a whole out of it.

I could ask her how to use a fork or a contraceptive and she would answer each one alike, immediately, definitely, simply and with authority. Now lots of people will try to do this for you. They will try so hard to be simple and direct and then, just to put you at your ease, they will turn right around and apologize for their knowledge by saying they probably don't know. This means that you have been through all the embarrassment only to have to ask somebody else because you do not have confidence in the answer.

You see, I was beginning to have a new and more satisfying concept of authority and to lay to rest the old one of the first chapter. My sister not only gave you the authority for your statements, but she had hers for her statements. All this tied in nicely with this new thing I was so enjoying in the zoology class—this having to give your authority if you made a quotation. The print was no longer enough. There was a live and human person behind the print, sometimes subject to error, but still you had to be meticulous about not leaving him out or getting him confused with another human being behind print.

I told my sister about the state I was in with my emotions. She did not deny it. She did not doubt that I had worked on it every day for six years. She did not think that it was a phase of adolescence (at least she didn't say so). She did not doubt but that it was serious, if I said it was. She did not laugh or think that it would automatically be cured by marriage. All these things she did not do, other people had done. I had tried to tell other people about this and *they thought I was boasting.*

Now I do not know just how she did it, but she very carefully planted in my mind an idea which was the key to the whole thing. I began to get the idea that while I was working with such discipline to stamp out the little fears, I was motivated by a bigger fear, that of being hurt. That what seemed to me courage was only *protection* and that it was, in fact, an unrecognized cowardice. She did not say it like that, you understand. I had the illusion, at least, of having figured it out myself.

But at the same time SHE DID NOT BELITTLE THE ACCOMPLISHMENT. It could be, I saw, a great accomplishment and still not be *good.* Now the very thing that was holding me back was my pride in those years of discipline.

She also said that Easy does it about coming out, and I know then that I would get out in plenty of time, and some time ecstasy would be mine.

I told my sister about the people I knew and she began to speak of Havelock Ellis, just as though Havelock Ellis and I were working together, hand in hand, on this problem. She automatically made it unnecessary for me to explain that I was neither motivated by morbid curiosity nor was I involved with any of them. Also, though she must have wanted to, she did not express any anxiety for my safety and she accepted my word for it that I was not being harmed by the twisted and ghastly things I was seeing.

And I told her about The Theory of Fundamental Rhythm, as I have said.

And I told her that I wanted to be a doctor. She did NOT remind me that I was a girl. She did NOT remind me of my health. She did not tell me that as soon as I got married I would get over all that. She did not act the way most people do, as though the entire matter of being a doctor consists of constantly cutting up dead bodies.

And if I had come to her the next week and said I wanted to be a musician she would have cut out her tongue before she would ever have said, Last week you wanted to be a doctor.

Yet this was not a studied technique with her. She did not go around indiscriminately telling people what they wanted to hear. There were a great many people whom she considered hopeless and weak and dishonest and on these she was inclined to be very severe. I knew this. That is why, when she took me seriously, it meant so very much.

Her husband treated me just as she did, too, and that also meant a great deal.

And, indirectly, she taught me my first real conception of tolerance. Bursting with ambition as I was, I questioned *her*. To me she was the wisest, most brilliant woman in the world. I had always thought that she would certainly be a very great writer, although she kept all her writing secret and would never let anybody see it, would, I think, as soon walk naked down Douglas Avenue as to see any of it in print. Yet she wrote the most beautiful letters that I ever read anywhere and I have seen a lot. I have read Vincent Van Gogh's, and my sister's are better.

She said, I do not want to do the big, brave things any more. Once I did. Now I want to sit back and watch other people do them. I do not want the big brave things. I want to be happy.

It sounded sad to me; it sounded like a compromise and I was almost ready to jump to the attack, the way that I was always going around jacking up other people's lagging ambitions, the way that I was always showering WILL on them and belief that they could *do*. But I was learning, you see. I kept still a little while. And then I looked at her and I did not want to change her in any way. I wanted her just the way she was, not greater or smaller, or taller or shorter, or anything but just the way she was.

And that is where I learned what tolerance is. Ah, sad word, badly mouthed about. How many thousands of times I had heard it lately, heard it whined out by my new acquaintances—God's little mistakes. What they meant when they asked for tolerance was license to continue whatever they were doing.

My sister told me about Caesar Franck. Perhaps it was earlier but if it was it sat in my mind because it was at this time that I got it. She told me of how he had lived out his life in obscurity, playing his beautiful works on the organ in an obscure cathedral when he could have been in the conservatory. She told me the difference between doing and being.

Ah, she told me so much. She listened to so much. She put my ego on a firm basis, where I no longer had to assert it to believe it was there. And it was the nearest thing I had ever had to communication. I thought it *was* communication, but it was not absolute. Yet, I still do not understand how she could do all the things she did with the differences between us.

True communication, as I learned later, is not only (from one side) listening to and absorbing the conclusions of another. It is also the following *of the mental processes* by which the conclusion is formed, and this is what is foreign to my sister. I do not mean that she cannot do it for you, though she has to try. It is that you cannot do it for her.   For my sister does not make a statement which, in its very *wording* lays open its own pathway so that you can see it. She does not know a thing because it is the fifth step in a series of five steps. She knows things like she knows her right arm. A telephone to her is not an extension of a human voice beyond the capabilities of the vocal cords. It is something which she will walk all over town to avoid using. Misfortune and tragedy are not to her means of gathering strength or are they ever classic in their literary potentialities. They are knots in her guts. They are ice in her stomach and IT IS NOT RIGHT THAT THEY SHOULD HAPPEN. Her sympathy is identical. If you have a pain she does not appreciate it; she *has* it. Grief to her is not lessened with the passage of time.* It stays constant or it

---

*As I wrote this I noticed a classical example of communication. Reading that passage *you* will *know* that I could not have said lessened with Time,

grows and there can *never* be a speaking of it. For my sister, there are a lot of things for which there are no words. For me, what I do not have a word for, I do not know.

Well, I read this over and I see how I have failed again. I have made a kind of picture of my sister as a benevolent female Jesus who has descended with her kindness and her wisdom and her graciousness to save me in the nick of time. I tried to write her in PEOPLE ARE GRASS, too, and utterly failed; I think I even hurt her.

Is it not sad that I can meet a strange old farmer on a bus and write such a tender portrait of him as GUARANTEED and I cannot give you a picture of my sister whom I have loved above all people? Not to a lover or a husband or a child can I give this particular, pure unquestioning kind of worship—and yet my portraits of her are always wrong.

In PEOPLE ARE GRASS she was austere.

In YOU WILL REMEMBER BUT STRANGELY she was hysterical.

In THE WAY THINGS ARE she was indefinite.

And in this she is a kind of gentle Jesus.

I think of the man who wrote R.F.D. and of how he said he once wrote a portrait of his wife which he was so very proud of and upon which he worked so long and of how not only his wife but ALL of her friends said that it was absolutely brutal and ruthless.

I think of Havelock Ellis's autobiography and of how when he gets through writing about Edith Lees all you wonder is how the hell he ever loved her.

And I think I will try again. Her hair is like mine, only it is almost red. Her head is much larger than mine. Her forehead is in three planes.

That does not do it and I am going to fail again. Let me humiliate myself still further. Her eyes are very large and of a clear shade of light blue. They are the most intelligent eyes you have ever

---

because Time is an abstract force and is not concerned with lessening. The *passage* of Time, not *Time*, is what I meant, so that is what I must say and as you read that, all this goes through your mind. Is it not so?

seen and they are not round, the way large eyes usually are, nor do they protrude. The upper lids have a distinct angle. You must be in hysterics by now. I will leave it, only adding that she is taller than I and very slender. (No diagram even attempted).

What I want to tell you is her gaiety and her quickness. Oh, she is so quick. She clicks clicks clicks her heels when she walks and if you drop something she can catch it before it hits the floor. And she laughs a great and wonderful laugh with her mouth open and she cries the biggest tears you ever saw without getting her eyes red and she was the first person who had any conception of what noises sound like to me when I am ill.

We never had enough time to say all the things and so we fell mentally into a kind of telegraphic language. We never planned this; we just fell into it. To say that in this language we eliminated all the adjectives and adverbs and all the little words (whatever they are called; I never learned any grammar) does not begin to tell you what hilarious situations such a language will provoke.

We have at various times also spoken in a language called alfalfa whilfich colfonsilfists ilfin pulfutting an l alfafter a vowelfowel, repeating the vowel with an f in front of it.

Before alfalfa we had pig Latin.

And in any language, always, we had laughter and pantomime and ridiculous situations.

One of these is this. My sister and I were walking down a business district alley in order to carry on a conversation which was constantly being interrupted by the people we knew on the streets. A garbage truck was parked very close to a building. My sister was ahead. She walked right by the truck without looking in. Abreast of the truck I, of course, looked in. There sat a monkey chained to the steering wheel.

Hello, I said to the monkey.

He flew straight at my face and let me have it, scratching the right eyelid. I backed off, holding my eye, went around the truck on the other side. Here sat another monkey. I did not say a word to him. He got the other eye. My sister and I stood there in the alley, with the blood streaming down my face, having hysterics because she had said, That could happen only to you.

Well, I think now, if I could tear all this out and start over about my sister, what would I tell you?

Here I am, a writer, a writer who is absolutely confident that she will some day write a great book, a writer who will attempt no compromise, who will try for no small safe goals, a writer who, in the privacy of her own boudoir, is sometimes not ashamed to say that she is trying to be with Milton and with Joseph Conrad and with Thomas and part of Carlyle. Here I am that writer and I mean to tell you about my sister and I think a long time and finally I come out with this eloquent piece of writing, this great creation, this amazing never-before-expressed expression:

She is good. She is beautiful. She is gay.

So I give it up. I can only pay her little, and doubtful, compliments. Almost always my feminine characters' names begin with E.* And when I write a really good one (perhaps THE GREEN KINGDOM) I shall use the whole name, Erma.**

And I gave her the original of TURNIP'S BLOOD written in longhand in a little book like this, with an orange cover.

And sometime I will do for Robin what she did for me, because his mind is so much like mine that I could find my way around in it without a light and barefooted.

But this is not a book about my sister. This is a book about a search for communication and of how I abandoned the search for self-sufficiency and of how, seeing the self-sufficiency as a deep well with a high wall around it, I wanted out.

There was the girl who loved Howard. She made me see that it was desirable to *get* out. There was my sister, who showed me what was keeping me in. And there were all the new things in school (at last difficult enough to be interesting) which gave me

---

*I think this also has something to do with FRANCES and FRANCIS.
**I have her permission for this.

something to do besides sit around and experiment on my mind. There was The Theory of Fundamental Rhythm and there was organic chemistry. I was not even a brilliant student in this, only average, and yet I was thrilled, truly thrilled by it. It was, as I remember, the synthesis of the amino acids that got me the most excited, the logical building up step upon step. It was like evolution.

There was a fine time in the comparative anatomy class when the teacher was outlining the cranial nerves of the shark. She described each one briefly and when she came to the last, said that no one had, as yet, dissected out the last one, nor explained its function. I was overcome by excitement, just at the thought of attempting this. The whole nerve was not more than three inches long, yet it took me three days to dissect it. One of those days was Saturday and one was Sunday. I have rarely been so happy. If the nerve had an analagous function to the form just below it, then I knew by its function where it SHOULD be. That's where it went. It was so logical and so simple I still do not see why it had not been done before. The nerve however was white; so were the muscle fibres and because it had all worked out so logically, I did not believe it when I saw it. I could not believe that I had done it. So I tore down the other side and found it again and dissected it out.

And not a single fibre broke.

Yet I was not a careful person. I rarely handed in a paper that did not have a blot on it. My drawings were sloppy and inaccurate and I was not even noted for my personal neatness, beyond cleanliness; for my hair was wild and unconfined and I could never resist picking up stray dogs and cats and sitting down on whatever was handy when I was tired.

But on my own, I could be neat and careful and whatever was necessary. The teacher said, That was a good piece of work. And I have never had such fine praise.

Later in another school I had a fine day. It grew out of a Greek sculpture class. I set the frieze on the Parthenon to music. I derived a constant measure for the vertical differences between

head heights of the figures in the frieze and this constant I repre-
sented by one note. The same applied to the hands. There was a
line of notes for the height of the heads

and one for the hands. The value of the note was determined
by the horizontal distances between the figures, as measured
against that between the two closest. And put together, the heads
line and the hands line, you know what it played?

It played a gentle, lovely melody exactly like a hymn!

Later on in medical school there were hundreds of wonderful
days—days that simply went by unobserved while I was lost in
what I saw under a microscope. There was the day when I held
under my hand what makes a human face. When I measured with
my own hands this thing called beauty or ugliness or good or evil
or Chinese or English—and it is less than an inch thick!

It is a thin sheet and it has molded how many lives, warped
how many personalities, this tiny fraction of the body's weight.
By this tiny sheet, a woman had caused armies to fight and because of it, another had been all her life apologetic and unsure.

And I had respect for the bodies and I kept them covered, not
out of sentimentality, but because I could not believe it could be
done for mine unless I did it for another's, the way that I must
always treasure and protect and care for whatever small things I
have that once belonged to a person now dead, so that it will be
possible for me to believe that someone will take care of my
things—will not let the dust be in my teacups, will not let the
moths eat my red tablecloth with the white deer on it, will not
cover up the head of my teddy bear, nor ignore my dog.

And there was the time when I sought for the truth between
sound and color and when I found a constant with which to
multiply sound waves so that they would come out near definite
light waves and from this I set Tschaikowsky's Andante Cantabile
(Vth) to color.

And there was the day that I learned concrete exercises for

thinking. This happened in a parasitology class and it may be that the teacher said it in so many words. I don't know. Anyhow, if you have heard students recite in any class where they are called upon to describe what they have seen, you know in what a maze of indefiniteness they flounder. How they will never WAIT to choose the right term but will use anything that approximates it in order to get to the end. How they are absolutely firm in the belief that they *can see* something and still not be able to describe it. How they believe that a mind is able to have a general impression of something. How, in the worst floundering, they are more than eager to credit the listener with already knowing what they are trying to say. And how they will go on and on like this, never disciplining themselves, never *waiting* for a word, always believing that they can know a thing which they cannot put into words or cannot draw.

I was doing it, too, of course, and then I had this idea (as I said, the teacher may simply have said it). To imagine that there were some kind of recording device or camera which would only portray before your eyes what you said, as you said it.

Imagine yourself describing a particular tree. This tree is a tall, cylindrical column of compact cellulose. The recording device draws this: You forgot to say that it was a vertical column. You repeat. The recording device straightens up the column. From its upper extremity project three large branches (also cylindrical but smaller than the trunk in diameter) one of which is forked.

The recording device adds: These large branches give onto smaller branches

 Which, in turn give onto many very small twigs.

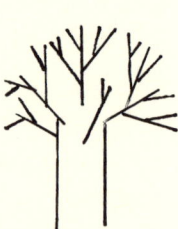

So you think you've done pretty well. Now you imagine looking at the imaginary picture which the imaginary recorder has produced. You have omitted

(1) the leaves
(2) the bark
(3) the arrangement by which the branches come out of other branches
(4) the angle at which the branches come off.

You have also omitted the tree's kind, function, and roots, but that is excusable because you were only describing what you could see.

But most people say, A tree, you know what I mean. And are done with it.

This imaginary recorder or camera was a great thing for me. I would do exercises with it. I would describe a lawn mower, an egg beater, a chair, a teacup, as though to a blind man—or to a person who had never seen these things. It was fine and satisfying discipline because if you will wait for the right word it will always come, and because you learn right away that the fault is not in your descriptive abilities, but in your observation.

And the habits hold over into the telling of ideas and the description of sensory impressions which can only be done in terms of something else; as it is no good to describe a shade of green to a blind man by telling him its rate of vibration. You have to say it is like eating celery.

These were the good days in school, among others, and the obvious thing is how little the thoughts had to do with the classes.

Yet they sprang from the classes.

A writer needs always and constantly many springboards for the imagination, and this is where many of them make their mistakes. They think that art is capable of reproducing itself, that you will paint from seeing paintings, or write from studying writings, but it is not so.

The tenth book must go back to the beginnings and be born from the source the same way the first book was. You cannot produce it out of the ninth book.

There is plenty as does, I know, but I am only talking about real books.

But lumping the good school days together this way, I am getting ahead of myself; for in the days of the observation exercises I was already OUT.

Let us go back to the first college and to the day that I came home and asked my father if he had any money in the bank. He said he had about $200.00. I asked him if I could have it. He said that I could if I needed it. I said I needed it. He said what for. I said that I limped and that it was by now impossible for me even to make a pretense in the gymnasium classes and that without the credit from these classes I could never graduate. He put down his newspaper and said, Walk across the floor. I did. By God, you do, he said. And he asked me what I was going to do about it. I had the surgeon and the hospital already chosen because I was not going to be played around with by any more quacks and I had found out how to tell the good ones.

I had found a surgeon who operated on the very poor children and I knew that it is only the great who will give of their knowledge and their art and their talents and their time to the poor. The lesser ones give them money.

My mother was all for having me run down to see Doctor So and So, who was, as a matter of fact, a good doctor, but I was not taking any more chances.

My father said to my mother, Let her go where she wants to. It is *her* back.

That is why I had to stand in silence all those years while he went again and again to a notorious quack to have removed from his face and hands, singly, some forty non-malignant tumors which he believed to be cancer, since they looked to him exactly like the cancer which he had watched kill his brother. That is why I had to stand by in silence and watch him pile up needless scars on his face and his beautiful hands, because, it was his face, and I could do no less for him than he had done for me.

It was in the hospital, in a cast from my neck to my ankles, free from pain for the first time in eight years, that I saw . . .

The Fly

It was to this doctor that I at last put up a battle for the chance of describing the attacks which had been occurring over a period of five years or so.

The first one had occurred in a public place and I had been carried home. My father was very frightened and had immediately called a doctor. My mother diagnosed the case for the doctor and did all his work for him and told him I had fainted (this also was explained by adolescence. Ah, poor maligned state). We repeated this performance several times and, since the attacks were always over by the time the doctor got there, the mistake is excusable. I could hardly expect the doctor to take the word of a very young girl against that of her mother and I did not put up a very good fight, but I knew that I did not faint, because I had seen people faint and they went down slowly. Also, I would be so stupefied that I could not possibly have explained the accompanying mental aberrations.

Would anybody believe me if I told them that I could hear the touch of linen, of velvet, of satin? That to touch my hair would produce a deafening racket? That the world looked two dimensional like a postcard and the design on the wallpaper stuck out in relief from the wall? But mainly, that the smallest detail of an inanimate object (an upholstering button or the texture of cloth) was filled and overflowing with pathos and with significance? That light was yellow and fluid as honey and dripping blindingly from all things? And that nothing seemed familiar and I was lost, lost, lost?

You do not know how to say these things when you are little.

By the time you try, they are gone and you do not believe them yourself.

But if the attacks were bad, the time following was worse. They WATCHED me. My father's eyes would watch every gesture. If I stumbled ever so slightly, he would be on his feet and over to me within a second.

They did not usually happen at home and so I got so I would stay away until I could walk home and then go straight to bed. Or I would hide them anyway I could in order to avoid hearing my mother sit down and explain them all away, in order to avoid the fright in my father's eyes. So it is not unusual that my mother underestimated them because she did not know how many there had been.

But I had found an *authority* now in whom I had confidence and I did not mean to be put off. Oh, the relief of having someone know what I was talking about.

This is more serious than your back, he said, and when you are in the hospital I will get you a good neurologist and he will know all about it.

No more were we outside the door than my mother turned on me. Why did you tell him those things? she said. They have nothing to do with your back. He will think you have *fits*.

Maybe I do, I said. I looked at her, so beautiful, so stately, so firm, and I did not understand her yet.

I looked at her and I remembered the long, long line of little subterfuges and hypocrisies and glossings of the truth, and protection, and hiding. How when I was little she was always cautioning me not to enter so violently into a relationship with a playmate, lest I be hurt. Not to see one so often, lest I become tired of her. (But there are *plenty* of children, I had said to her then. If one wears out I will get another.) How her whole criterion of what was suitable and sufficient underwear was based on the possibility of a street accident which would necessitate one's being taken to the hospital. How the first thing she did when my father's rages began was to close all the windows so that the neighbors should not hear. How the women she had known for twenty years, she still called by their last names. How, upon finding cigarettes in my brother's pockets, she had sat down and convinced herself that he did not smoke.

I did not understand her yet and I hated her methods and I knew once and for always that they could never be mine.

The neurologist came and he talked with me for a long time. He asked how long the attacks lasted and I said about two hours. He told me they could not possibly have lasted more than two minutes. (Oh, Time, I thought I knew you so intimately).

My own theory for them was that they were caused by my having meddled around with my emotions, that by stifling them I had refused them an outlet for their energy and that finally this energy would accumulate until it burst out in this form. I told him about the long years of self-sufficiency and he said that it was an interesting theory and that I had thought it out very logically. Only, what I was describing was hysteria and what I *had* was petit mal.

By this time I had come to be quite ashamed of the self-sufficiency and the damage I thought I had done myself.

But isn't it what we are all trying to do? he said, very mildly. Are we not all of us trying one way or another to be in some degree the masters of our fate, not to be merely the victims of our own temperaments?

I told him about the conquering of the fears and he pointed out to me so easily that most of them were based on noise. Isn't it strange that I had never made this extra little step? That the trains had remained trains and the sand, sand, and my father's swearing, swearing? Isn't it strange that I had been able to go so far and had never been able to go this little step further, to find a common denominator for them?

He told me about many other cases like my own, so that in this way I could understand my own. He very mildly and slowly and easily robbed them of their mystery and their shame and their need to be hidden and he lessened the likelihood of their progressing into something larger than I. He said that I knew better how to take care of myself than anyone he had known. He said that I was not to take another's estimate of my strength or my limitations and that he thought I would be able to do whatever I wanted to. He said he saw only one grave danger to me, one way that I could be destroyed and thwarted and changed into what I did not want to be and that was if I should have the misfortune to fall in love with someone far inferior to me in intelligence.

I could not wish for a creative child a greater blessing than a serious illness before twenty.   A time of contemplation and of QUIET is essential to the flowering and is almost impossible to achieve in daily life. What you have never had you cannot imagine as necessary.   Not until stillness is FORCED on you in some way, do you realize its value, do you know enough to ask for it.

I had to lie absolutely still because I was fixed up so that I could not move. I felt better than I had ever felt and I was gradually changing my measurements of time, this inevitable accompaniment of the hospital, so clearly described in Mann's THE MAGIC MOUNTAIN. For the minutes no longer matter, only what happens, and the activity is not going on where you can point to it; it is going on in your head and here it will not record itself in the way that you were used to. Gradually, gradually, I was slowing down. I was getting still. I was getting quiet. I was being carried by the current where the stream is broader.

A little fly came in the window. He sat upon my chest. Out of habit I started to brush him off. How silly, I thought, to go batting around with your hands and frightening the fly when the reason for doing so has been eliminated; for there was a good inch and a half of cast between the fly and my skin and though he stamp his feet and walk and dance and tickle, I could not feel him.

I looked at the fly.

It was the first thing I ever really saw.

He had green eyes and fine hairs upon his feet and beautiful wings and, in no hurry, I lay and watched him for an hour.

I did not try to impress upon him my personality. I did not try to fit him into a preconceived idea of my own. I did not even try to make him a representative of the animal kingdom as the insects or all flies. I did not think at all.

I was quiet and I watched the fly, this one particular fly, and I did not know beforehand what I was trying to learn.

I *saw* the fly.

And when my nurse came into the room, I *saw* her. And when I was released from the hospital I stood on a street corner WATCHING the people. No two of them were alike. I did not have a book under my arm and I was not in any hurry.

I would never run for a street car again or measure accomplishment by quantity or miss the value of idle moments by trying to improve them, and when a human being spoke to me I would not be interested only in explaining and interpreting what he said. I would listen to *how* he said it.

For in life, even as in literature, the PLOT is NOT the thing.

I was ready and able now to COME OUT (how symbolically is this term used for debutants!) and I had prepared myself. All I needed now was. . .

Love

With neither practice nor seeking I found it. The minute I saw him, without reason or logic, I loved him, but he was famous and important and older than I and I thought that this must happen to him with every young girl; so I would not look into his eyes, lest he see it.

For his part, which I learned later, the fact that I would look only over his head while he spoke to me he interpreted as boredom. It must have been very disconcerting and it made him speak in very jerky sentences. This I thought was his impatience WITH me.

This went on at intervals for a year. You wonder how we ever managed to get together.

Then one day by accident our hands touched. Instinct is not confused. It does not misinterpret. He asked me to meet him. I did and we went for a long walk together. He was carrying my school books, a thing to which he was not accustomed, and he kept dropping them. While we walked a strange drugged state overcame me. I was walking a foot off the ground wrapped up in cellophane. Through the cellophane began to penetrate new impressions of the places we were seeing. We were passing houses that I passed every day and did not notice. Now I began to notice all the human stories behind these houses. In one a man had committed suicide many years before. That fact no longer meant to me a crowd and people talking and mystery. It meant a man's despair. In all of them the same.

He asked me to have dinner a month later. Many times during the month I did not believe he had asked me. I did not believe that he would remember it. But we both did. We were both punctual, though he was there first. We were going to have dinner in a hotel dining room and neither of us had known a month before that there would be a convention of fishermen in this hotel. We walked through the lobby, slowly and with difficulty, surrounded on all sides with the very symbols of unreality. On all sides there were huge glass tanks filled with clear green water and swimming in these were strange marine forms, giants and small ones and ones with streamers. As I threaded my way through the crowd, I would look from side to side and each time catch the great blank questioning eye of a fish that I had never seen.

We came to feel that we were swimming through the water, slowly floating under the green water among the silver bubbles, in a green watery blur of sound.

It was all fantastic and unreal and eating, it was much worse, because the fishermen were so very gay and so very numerous. Across the table, we could not hear each other speak. I had thought constantly of this meal for a month and then, when it was there, I could not eat it.

He was so concerned with my not being able to eat and he begged me to think of something, of anything, that I could eat. I thought a long time and finally I said, Spinach. He got it and I ate it and it tasted very good. I was thoroughly convinced of the powerful transformations wrought by love, because I did not like spinach.

There we sat in the midst of the boisterous, shouting, laughing, fishermen, I slowly eating my lovely spinach in infinitesimal bites. And we could only look at each other. It was a maddening situation. Finally, he said, I cannot stand this noise any longer. I did not know they would be here. It is usually so quiet here. If you would trust me, he said, we could go to my room and talk.

I thought that we would, I said.

I sat in a chair and he sat on the floor, smoking his pipe. We now had quiet and no words to speak. I do not know how long we sat so. Finally he leaned over and kissed my feet and said, I love you profoundly.

And all the threads which had held me for so long so tightly bound together—they all snapped. I knew that their loose ends would be flying all about the room as soon as the center began to whirl. There was a crack in the wall of the dam and soon the wall would crumble and the waters roar through. But I was used to being alone, to thinking alone, and to crying alone. I did not know how to break the dam with him there. I asked him to leave me alone for ten minutes and he said he would.

I turned out the lights and sat down on the floor by the window in the dark and I let it break. Ah, here were they all, all the old things—floods of them, roaring and sweeping and taking possession. I had not killed them then. My emotions. They were not dead, but (as some old dame always remarks at funerals) only sleeping.

You know how it would be in a hurricane country, how with the warning you must board up all the windows and the doors. Then the air inside the room becomes unbearable and you are only going to open one tiny little slat, just to let in a breath of air.

And there the whole hurricane is inside the room before you can do a thing.

They were all back, just as though the years of self-sufficiency had never been, the years of discipline. Six, seven, eight years shot to hell. Here was the girl who was afraid of nothing, who felt nothing. A man kissed her feet and said, I love you profoundly, and he was the right man and he gave her a word to go on.

Now you could scare me to death with a fire engine siren. You could put Garbo up in front of me and let her say, I love you, and I would bawl like a baby. She didn't need to say anything. Just let her stand here and I will weep for she is beautiful and her brow is noble. It doesn't even have to be Garbo. Let the scrawniest most awkward shop girl stand there. Let me look at her and I will weep; for I know that in the secret chambers of her heart she carries a picture of herself in which, also, she is beautiful and her brow is noble.

Oh, come on you beggars and street peddlers and work worn cart horses. Come on you con men and fake sword swallowers. Here is a sucker, full blown and newly arisen, good for a touch to the end of her days.

A man kissed my feet and said, I love you profoundly, and he was the right man and he gave me a word to go on.

All this took only a little while; for when he came back I was quiet. He sat on the floor beside me, in the dark, high above the city in a little room, and we did not speak at all. And outside, the great soft feathered wings of time flapped slowly by. I could hear Time moving by, but with a difference. Though still abstract, impersonal, and unconcerned, it was no longer malevolent—and it was SLOWING DOWN.

He was beautiful, the most beautiful man that I have ever seen. He was slight and all his joints were neatly and smoothly articulated. In the smallest gesture he was exact and graceful and utterly confident. To see him take a cigarette from his case and light it is so beautiful and exact that it would break your heart. He ties a shoe lace in three motions, never any more. Never any less.

He was patient, infinitely patient, and he waited for Time to slow down. He would hold my hand and sometimes touch my eyelids. And he was infinitely patient.

He gave me back my childhood. He was thirty years older than I and to him this was a disadvantage, a barrier. He had no idea how delicious it was for me to be younger than someone I knew, to be offered protection; for always always everybody thought there was no limit to my energy, no limit to the trouble I could listen to.

He gave me my childhood. I began to read fairy tales. Hans Christian Anderson and Alice in Wonderland and hundreds of others. And one day, by myself, I laughed for no reason.

It was laughter for its own sake. It was simple, unexplained, uncaused joy.

I loved him beyond myself. I desired his happiness more than anything on earth. Then he began to suffer battles of conscience about the difference in our ages. (Had I not always, always, been on a bad footing with Time?) He would go away for weeks at a time and he would send me away, but always we came back. He discussed and exploited and lectured me on all the various possible angles of this barrier and he never never understood how it was an advantage to me. Finally he promised that if I was still with him in five years he would quit lecturing me. He would quit talking about it, but the very day it was five years he forgot and spoke of it again. He has never been reconciled. It has always seemed to him that he did me a great injustice.

Yet he gave me all the good things, all the fine things I had.

He gave me a childhood.

And sudden laughter.

And joy.

And faith in a human being's goodness.

And patience.

And an understanding of domesticity.

And kindness.

And gentleness.

And because I could love him so deeply, so fully, other people began to love me and I no longer aroused hatred or resentment in them. Because I had seen him I could see others. I could tell by looking at people now, their needs. I could tell if they were tired or worried or frightened.

He gave me their faces.

And I wanted to be surrounded with good and decent people. I wanted to be in the sunlight. I wanted to be happy. I went home and burned all my case histories and in one day I stopped seeing all the maladjusted and the abnormal people I knew, because in five years, their stories had lost their great interest and their variety and I began to be aware that I was hearing over and over again the same things, that they would never reconcile their conclusions and their hypotheses. It was as though, always, they said, I steal things but I am not a thief. If you genuinely want to stop stealing things you must ultimately say, I am a thief and so I steal things, and then it will be possible for you to start over and not steal things.

And they so rarely really wanted help. They wanted a good audience. I understood their need but I had something better to listen to. I had the solemn proud thanksgiving of my heart.

But never let them tell you that love cannot exist of itself, that it has to be constantly nourished and fed with other things; for it is not true. Alone and unaided, if it is great enough, it lives upon itself. We had no experiences in common and I never met any of his friends and, except for Erma, he never saw any of mine.

Except for that first fantastic one among the fishermen we have never had a meal together. We have never been to a movie or walked in an orchard or danced together. We have never been swimming or mended a piece of furniture or had a quarrel.

I live in a house and when he can he comes there. Before he comes everything is scrubbed with soap, even in the corners, even in the places he will not explore and when he has to go, he leaves. I have never asked him why he was late nor asked him to stay when he had to leave. He has never asked of me the simplest thing and how I wish he would.

I am not necessary to him and I have always known it.

Yet we have loved each other deeply and profoundly and constantly for ten years.

Never let them tell you that you have to like the same books and know the same people. It is not so.

For this I abandoned the search for communication and this is where most people lose it forever, because they become absorbed in a constant round of continuous tasks. It is their tasks which they recite to you (the ones they have just done, the ones they are going to do) and this habitual recital serves the purpose to them of communication. Rarely do they remember the search. Sometimes on New Year's Eve or when they are sick or when they watch children playing you can see them remember the old quest. They could not tell you themselves what it is that flits across their mind, a short-lived feeling that they have missed somewhere, that they have been cheated.

And it would call to me sometimes in the night and sometimes from the pages of a book and sometimes from the eyes of a friend, but I had something more important. I had something better, and I would not listen.

He would come and I would wait and then he would come and again I would wait until he came again. And when he was not there I carried the thought of him around with me like a coat and I did not know that I was lonely.

We did not have communication and I never pretended that we did; for I never looked to find everything in one bundle. The things that I have thought out so long and so carefully, a thing like the conception of Time, for example, are precious to him. It occasions, I think, only the tenderest kind of amusement that I would stick so stubbornly to a quest such as the one for communication, that I could, at a moment's notice, tick off one two three four, the different stages in the search.

I can save up and treasure for him my anecdotes. I can see very accurately and I can remember and I can hear what is said exactly and remember the sound of each word as it was spoken, because I have trained myself to do these things. Well, I can come running to him with this perfect find of a thing seen and heard and if IT DOES NOT MAKE HIM THINK OF ONE THAT HE SAW LIKE IT. Nor does he thrill to see the angle of my observation and how consistently I have maintained it.

He sees my eyes, seeing.

I could figure out what makes the creatures of the world alive, I could be a source of strength to thousands, I could write the most wonderful, the truest book in the world, I could be the finest, most gentle, the biggest woman who ever lived and he would laugh very tenderly and pat me on the head. I am not his mother nor his wife nor his sister nor his friend nor his Virgin Mary nor his refuge. I am his precious childie and it will never change.

And I like it. It is a kind of immortality, a perpetual youth. I would not have him different than he is. Yet he has never asked a hundredth of what I have to give.

And have I missed the same with him I wonder? Have I ever been so wrong with him as he was about the ring? I wanted a ring. I wanted a ring to wear that he had given me. I did not care if it was made out of wire or cigar bands or had once held keys. I wanted, when I was alone, to be able to put on his ring and walk about my house wearing it, and he simply could not remember to get it.

Yet he can remember to bring me a book. He *never* forgets an appointment. He has remembered so many many things, but he simply could not remember to bring me the ring.

I did not like to nag him about it and so I kept thinking each time he came he would have the ring. Months went by and I thought he was saving it for a special time, for an anniversary, but the special times came and went. And I humiliated myself and I asked him again. I was sure he would bring it then, but it was to be a long time before he would come back. And in the meantime I could not wait; for I had imagined it so long and waited so long that I had become aware of that finger to the point where I could hardly make it function any more. It is like having a sore tooth.

You cannot think of anything else. The finger began to ache. I would wake up in the night and it would be aching. It hurt with aching the way you imagine a cow must feel left unmilked and her master dead. So, while I was waiting for him to come back, I bought myself a ring to pretend on. As soon as I would get home from work I would run and put it on and I would talk to it and my finger quit aching.

He came home and I could hardly wait. I thought that he was saving it, but he got ready to leave and he had said nothing and I turned on him and I said, You forgot my ring, and he said, Oh, my God, I did.

After that I thought for sure he would remember it, but he did not. My pretense ring was a mockery to me now and a constant reminder, yet it was such a part of me that I could not bring myself to throw it away. So finally I gave it to him and told him about it and begged him to throw it away for me, but he did not know but what it was valuable and he did not like the responsibility of carrying it about and he said,

Where did you get it?

And I remembered the day I bought it and how humiliating had been the clerk's eyes, how she had thought I must be buying it to fool a house detective in a momentary affair, and I said,

The dime store.

And he laughed and put it in his pocket and went away. And I was glad to be rid of it, but as the days went by, it occurred to me that now he would know the size and EVEN THEN I still half hoped that he would remember but he did not.

And it was two years since I had first asked him.

He simply could not remember to get it. There was no point in accusing him. Some people cannot bring themselves to write a letter. They simply cannot and that is all there is to it.

I think that that is all there is to it, and yet I do not know. He is sometimes capable of extreme subtlety and it is possible that he took the need for the ring as a sign of my need for a more concrete life than I had with him. He has always thought that my own instincts and my own chemistry would eventually betray me into a marriage with someone my own age. He is so utterly confident of Nature and her unrelenting processes and perhaps he is right. He wants very much to see me happily married, living a full and normal and many-sided life and perhaps he was using the ring to force me to recognize the needs of these things a little quicker. I have lived with him ten years and I do not know whether he thought all this out or whether he simply could not remember it. Is it not sad that two people so close cannot speak to each other any better than that?

I had abandoned the search for communication for a long time, but it would not stay hidden.

I had tried my father.

I had tried the children.

I had tried Tawm.

I had tried the imaginary baby.

I had tried Aileen.

I had tried my sister.

I had tried my lover.

And though I had tried many things and found many things different from and perhaps even better than communication, I had never found communication.

Well, I would try once again and this time I would find it. I would have a child. It would be my own child and we would talk together. I would not wait this time until the ears were unatuned, until the mold was set, until the fight to stay alive had dimmed the search. I would start from the beginning. And when the child spoke to me I would not turn my back to it and rattle pans. I would STOP and LISTEN. And when the child asked questions I would not give it a lot of careless sentences. We would find out the answers together, my child and I, one at a time as they came up. If the child asked me how does a telephone work and I did not know, we would go down to the telephone company together and make them show us. If the child said, Why did it rain today, I would never say because it was cloudy. We would go down to the weather bureau and we would find out. And the child should never live on any standards but its own and, as long as it was with me, it should never hear any lies.

But of course I could not have a child because I was not married. What strange biology is this? Was the species then governed by ceremony?

No, that was not true.

How now, little Rachel, are you afraid then?

I looked in my heart and I was not afraid.

I longed for a child and I hungered for a child and I wished the earth to be graced again with a face so beautiful as my lover's face and I hoped that it would happen while he was in Europe; for I knew that he would never believe me. He would never believe that I was truly emancipated from the world's standards. He would never believe that I lived upon my own. He would never believe that I was strong enough to stand out against the world without apology. He would never believe that the gifts of ATTENTION and of honesty and of courage that I had to give the child would make up to it for its being a bastard. And I was right, because later I tried to explain this to him and he would only listen with the world's ears and I got so bogged down at the impossibility of making him understand that I cried.

And he thought that I wept for myself.

He went to Europe and I told him goodbye. I was almost sure and I did not tell him.

And then I was sure and I wrote to him many letters and I did not tell him.

I was radiantly, gloriously, beautifully happy. I had no past and no future—only one beautiful moment in time. I was never sad nor frightened. Nor did I think or plan or ask advice. I lived in a blissful, vegetable state, without appendages.

I was a perfect circle.

I was a perfect sphere.

And I told no one, confided in no one. Not even my sister did I tell this. This was all mine and I did not think how unfair this was to my lover.

And I forgot about my back and I forgot that I had ever had an attack and I forgot that it was wicked to ask a child to do for you what you cannot do for yourself. I forgot that it was wicked to ask a child to live for any reason but its own.

There was Tawm and there was the imaginary child and there was Aileen and there was my son and they were all of them dead, one after the other, but I used no false names; for I was not ashamed. And yet I did not weep; for it must be true as they say that one weeps only for oneself, that in a friend's death one sees one's own.* I was not sorry for myself. I was grateful for all I had had. But I was sorry for my son and I said to him,

I am sorry for you, my son, that you will never see the green things growing in the spring nor ever love nor recognize your death.

For at the time these seemed to me the three great privileges of living.

I looked out the hospital window at the many trees and I looked at a little squirrel which had all through the long long day been running back and forth among the branches of the tree and that is the day I understood. . .

Abstraction

As I watched him the words kept running through my head, All the little warm things, all the little warm things, and I knew that I was close to something important; for there is more than a step or two in evolution between a fish and a bird; there is the greatest difference in the world. For a fish is the same temperature as his environment and his heart functions so perfectly that he is never aware of it, but with the warm things this is not so. With the warm things, the feathered and the furred and the skin covered, there is a difference between the body tempera-

---

*I do not really believe this.

ture and that of the environment and, fighting against this difference, is the heart. And through the chambers of the heart, the red blood flows, and because the difference is sometimes extreme and because the heart's function is not always the same so that it can always be forgotten and taken for granted, then are the warm things made to remember and recognize their own hearts. Then do they feel the flowing of the red blood through the chambers of the heart.

How many chambers has a squirrel's heart? How many chambers are there in the heart of a bird, a rabbit, a sheep, a goat? How many chambers are there in the heart of a man? Chamber within chamber, secret and hidden—how many chambers are there in a man's heart? These things I must know. I must know the number of the chambers of a squirrel's heart. The red blood flowing at different rates for different times through the chambers of a rabbit's heart or that of a bird or a cow or a sheep or any beast of the field or the air, must not be a secret from me. And I must know the hidden secret chambers of a man's heart, of all the men's hearts, one at a time. For it is here, flowing through the hidden chambers of the heart, that the red blood leaves the record on the wall, hangs its pictures on the wall. What are the pictures on the wall in the countless hidden chambers of a man's heart? Chamber within chamber. I must know them all, each one. How infinitely rich and purple and many textured are the pictures even in a bully's heart—in the secret hidden chambers of a bully's heart!

And from the concrete, small, and individual body of my son I gathered up the concrete, small and individual love that I had put there. I gathered it into a sphere and, still rounded with the imprint of my hand, I cast it out the window to the squirrel and it was molded in a sphere so that from the squirrel it should roll to the bird and from the bird to the rabbit and to all the warm things in the world.

For it was no longer necessary that a child to be mine should have been carried within my belly. I carried whatever creature is warm within my heart, for *whoever* gave it birth, I was its mother.

And after the sphere, I cast my maternity, out, out, out to the squirrel and the rabbit and the beasts of the fields and the creatures of the air and all mankind, one at a time.

And I became a mother in the abstract.

And after this I could understand abstract painting, as I never had been able to before. I had thought that it was different from and opposed to and at war with realistic painting, but it is not so. It is the *same thing in a bigger room*. Even with a realistic painting, if you stand far enough from it, it becomes almost an abstraction of itself.

I had not thought to see my house again and so I had left it clean and in order and thus it was waiting for me. There had been a day when I had heard continually the notes of Beethoven's fifth symphony in my mind and I was eager to get to the victrola so that I should hear it again, but it did not satisfy me and that day it sounded thin.

What I needed was something thicker and redder and more deeply flowing and that is the day that I truly heard and took for my own the music of the colored people. This music is sometimes called swing, sometimes called boogie-woogie, but these are not good names and they do not say it.

It is as though music for many thousands of years had taken its own pulse and counted it, just as a nurse counts your pulse, one, two, three, four, counting only the systole and being content. And then one day, music paused and took its pulse again and was no longer content; for it had heard this time the extra sound in between the beats. This was the sound of the diastole. The blood beat is not four but eight to the bar. It is not one, two, three, four, but one-a, two-a, three-a, four-a. It is not only the going out but the coming back. The foot is not a solid piece and each step has the ball and heel.

There are many of them who can play one-a, two-a, three-a, four-a and there are some who can play it twice as fast, onera, towera, threeera, fourera. And then there are the great ones. Johnson and Ammons and Tatum and Lewis and others. These are the ones who know that the going out is stronger than the coming back, the systole is louder than the diastole. The one is stronger than the ah. And beyond this they know that the coming back is not as quick as the going out and that there is an infinitesimal pause there, a silence, and they do not fill it with anything. If you are truly listening you are compelled to fill this silence yourself and this is what makes it great.

And beyond this they know that if you move your arm out in a circle and bring it back, the motion is still going *out* while you are bringing it back and if you move it out again the motion is still coming back while you are moving it out.

The systole and diastole are not distinct from one another. In each there is the echo of the other, though they are not quite even. In the going out there is the sound also of the coming back and in the coming back is the memory of the going out and there is an infinitesimal pause between them.

And beyond this they know that blood is red and thick and deeply flowing and its beat has not been in music before.

And I had from my beloved a new and deeper and more gentle love and he spoke less often of the difference in our ages.

And I took all my new found wisdom and my knowledge of these things and I went home to see

My Mother

And I said to my mother, Tell me about the farm and how it was when you were little, and she did not hear me and I said it again and she said, It was just a farm, like any farm, and I raised my voice and shouted and shouted at her until she stared at me with shock but, at last, with attention, and she sat down.

What is it you dream of all the time? I said, so that you could never listen to me? I got so I did not mind, I said. I got so that I rather liked your arrogance and the fact that you were not impressed by what I had to say, because I thought you had something better. What is this day dream into which you have retreated for so long, shutting us all out? Is it a *place*? I said. Is it a place where you go, the same every time?

No, she said, it is no particular place. It is not the same every time. It is just what will I have for dinner tonight and will there be a letter from your sister today and I ought to go up in the attic and air out that old trunk of your grandfather's.

Is that all it was? I said.

Yes, she said, about. Of course it is different on different days.

For no more than *that*, I said, you turned your backside to me and rattled pans when I came to tell you of my great theories? For no more than that you could not hear me when I asked you to tell me about the farm so many times?

I did not think you were interested, she said.

Why would I ask you again and again if I had not been interested?

I did not think you really meant it, she said.

But how could you tell? I asked. You did not even *listen*.

Well, she said, I did not dare to listen to all of you. Your father and all of you, always getting nervous and mad and different every day. If I had listened to you all, I would have been as crazy as the rest of you. There had to be somebody, she said, in the house who could stay calm and the same every day in order to hold it together.

It was so wonderful to hear her speaking so frankly for the first time in her life and I began to laugh and she did too.

Well, she said, I had to do something and that is what I did. I got so I could sit right in the middle of all of you and never hear a word you said.

And I saw us all through her eyes and how ridiculous we all were, how we were always making a great fuss and bother about the smallest thing. And I laughed again and she did too.

And tell me about the farm, I said.

And she began. As she went on she would think of more and in the morning when I woke up she would have another story that she thought of in the night. And they simply rolled out of her, these simple beautiful stories, and each one pure art without sentimentality or interpretation—the real thing. About pigeons and corn silk dolls and riding bareback on horses and a playmate named Ruth Coates and an imaginary playmate and her brother John and having her ears pierced for ear rings. And they came on steadily for days, being now only the pure essence from fifty years' distilling in silence.

Not once in all these years had she dared to compete against my father's glamour as a raconteur, for there was such a difference in their stories. In my father's stories he was always the hero or else the character he knew best was, but in my mother's stories only Life or Death or Fate or Time or Nature was victorious.

And oh, the waste of it, the sad sad waste of it, of this beautiful healthy woman with all those wonderful stories in her living year after year by her pride and what she called dignity a continual compensation for the fact that she had not been born in a city— living in silence.

Feeding the animals which we brought home and forgot, cooking the food which we forgot to taste, making the beds upon which we tossed, waxing the floor upon which we paced, filling our rooms with flowers which we did not smell.

And against all of it, only one weapon—the long walks that she took by herself. And even there she had to fight, for my father thought the neighbors would think that he did not give her money for taxi fare. Once they were teasing each other and my father said he did not understand how she could just walk, with no direction and no goal.

You will stub your toe and break your neck sometime, he said, the way you go round with your head in the air.

I would as soon break my neck from stubbing my toe as to split my head open because I butted it into a wall, she said; for it was true my father looked at his feet when he walked and never ahead of him.

And I could walk either way now, either up or down or with direction or aimlessly. I could walk with them both now.

And tell me about the farm, I said, and she would begin at a new place, wonderful stories, rolling, rolling out, and I came to know her very well.

I sat and watched her sitting beside my father in the days while he died and as my father got closer to death the bony structure of his face began to assert itself little by little and he began to look a year younger with each breath, for only the covering changes—the bones remain young. And as my father's face began to go back through the years, my mother went back with him.

And when he died she did not look grief stricken or tired or haggard or a week without sleep. She was radiant and she looked exactly like a bride and she spoke to my dead father,

You were always so jealous of Marshall Steele and now you are both dead and I am still alive. Isn't that strange?

And I went outside the hospital room and I stood guard at the door so that she could be alone with him and she sat in there by his side talking, talking to my father.

Now that his eyes could not see her, now that his ears could not hear her, now that his lips could never speak to her again, she could at last tell him all the things she had had in her heart these many years.

And when she came out of the room I said, He had beautiful legs, didn't he? And she looked at me with gratitude; for I wanted her to know that I knew that grief is a physical thing and in the beginning it is the body that cries out and for a long time it cries alone. And I wanted her to know this so that she would not have to go even the first step to be in character—even the first step of the world's pretense that because you are a mother and a grandmother and your hair is white and people give you their seats on streetcars, that it is in any way different for your beloved to die than it would have been at any other time.

She was like a bride for a long time, young and dependent and shy about everything and then slowly she began to go back through the years again. There was a time when I know she was pregnant again, carrying her first child and there was a time when we were all in school and after that it began to go faster.

When she had reached her own age again she wrote to me, You be the mother now and let me be the child. I am tired.

But I am ahead again, for my father was still alive when I wrote

Turnip's Blood

I was not writing, was not studying writing, was not thinking about writing, never meant to write and I began to hear words spoken out loud. I naturally took them for an hallucination and rather welcomed them as a change from the ringing bells to which I was accustomed. But they would not be put down and they would not be ignored and they repeated and repeated until, to get rid of them, I wrote them down. As soon as one sentence was got rid of in this way another took its place. Finally it stopped. I read over what I had written and thought it was very funny and I wondered what it meant. A few weeks later it began again just where it had left off—the same names, the same people. A few weeks later again. Each chapter represents a separate night at intervals of several weeks. No word was ever chosen or changed. When the voice did not come back anymore that was the end.

When I read it over it amused me very much. I typed it off and sent it to my sister and told her how it had happened. She said I did not have to explain it, to go sit in the sun or eat a steak and leave it to her.

It was published and I had no idea that the process would repeat itself, nor could I start it at will. Because it was published I met George and Savvy and you did not meet me until after they had done their work and so you do not know how very much I have to be grateful for to them both. They were not interested in me because I was strange or because I was strong or because of the reasons that other people were. They liked me because I was simple and because I was honest and because I was straight forward and because I could sit so still. And they thought I was a writer. I would never have been able to say I was a writer when people asked me what I did. I said I worked in a paint store. And if I so much as wrote a line on paper and could not resist showing it to you to read, I would suffer the most horribly embarrassing anguish until you had spoken your first words. They gave me confidence and they made me feel important and they very slowly and easily and delicately made me feel that it was all right for me to say I was a writer. These little paragraphs—how can I tell you their tremendous importance?

And to George I became almost essential. It was wonderful to have him bring to me each night his triumphs and they were not in numbers—how *much* he had done that day or how *many* things—they were times when he had been decent and times when he had not been afraid and times when he had listened patiently to a long dull story for the sake of hearing underneath it a short and interesting one.

They taught me what and where a woman's kingdom is and I rejoiced to be in it. They gave me confidence and a little power and a feeling of importance and of being necessary.

I had in a way a tiny little circle of fame and it was sweet. This little circle was gathered around one afternoon and they began to question me about Turnip's Blood. They asked me why I had written a certain line and what a certain phrase meant and I was panic stricken, absolutely panic stricken, for I had never studied writing and I did not have the vocabulary for lying about it. I had my back against the wall and I finally said, I don't know what it means. I heard it spoken out loud by a voice and I copied it down. And I blushed scarlet because I was sure that they would all know immediately that it was an hallucination and that it was only a symptom of the attacks—the awful, stupid way that I had heard people explain Van Gogh's painting entirely by his epilepsy.

After the people were gone, Savvy said, You don't have to be embarrassed about the way you write. It's just the inspirational method, that's all. The Bible was written that way and Blake wrote that way. Lots of people write by inspiration and some write by composition and some mix the two methods.

Really? I said.

And it was not long until I was writing again. I wrote MOTHER OF A CHILD there and WE ARE EACH OTHER'S CHILDREN and a NO SPECIAL HURRY and a long, long poem called DECRESCENDO, and all these in a few months, and I got so I could take them to George and Savvy quite easily and listen to what they said.

The days went by without being counted and I was happy and in a kind of dream and I was important to George and I could talk to all the people who came there, Georgie Stoll and John Hammond and Milt Gross and anyone who came there easily and directly.

And it was a terrible temptation to stay there forever and then I began to see its dangers, I began to understand the many nervous breakdowns around me and the alcoholics and the people trying, trying to beat Time.

For no one can stand out against flattery and being taken seriously forever and I knew that in six months I would begin to believe that I was a genius and I would secretly doubt if I was really earning what I was being paid, but by this time I would have accumulated a series of possessions and the competitive spirit.

And I knew I must take my new confidence and my new happiness and my new stillness and my new stories and go home *where I knew who I was* while I waited for the maturation.

And then one day very near the last George said, I want you to meet a wonderful man. He talks just like you do and his name is. . .

John

I was to meet you and we were to go together to a broadcast and after that we were to meet George and then all of us were to go to your house for dinner.

And I heard your voice then for the first time. Never anywhere have I heard a voice so dramatic and yet it was very low—always very low, gaining almost its entire effect with no help from volume, very little from range—almost completely by timbre. Pronouncing the simplest words about the most commonplace subjects—it is always and constantly *charged* with life.

And you got your camera and we got in your car and we started off. There had been a great many last minute details in your office and we were in danger of being late to the broadcast. All this had made you very nervous. You said, I just need five minutes and I will be all right.

So I had a chance to see your face. Well, not a beautiful face at all the first time you see it—the eyes always tired and overworked. The mouth though is very fine, not large lips but such very mobile ones because, of course, the diction is always, always perfect and very distinct and without the mobility of these lips this is not possible.

But all these things completely blotted out and lost, once you have seen that brain box. There it sits atop the face so obviously what it is used for. With odd bumps and lines on it it shines forth, simply overhanging everything else. It overhangs the eyes and it overhangs the ears and it overhangs the back of your head. It is not to be ignored and it is impossible to take one's eyes from it.

Well, in the car you kept asking me questions and I would answer yes or no and this bothered you very much. Finally you said, I am having a hard time finding a subject that strikes you.

---

*Truthfully he said Jack and it was not until after several letters to me that suddenly you signed one John so that for a special relationship you should have a special name.

And I said, I am giving you your five minutes.

You simply stared. How many thousands of times had you said at the end of the day, I need five minutes, and everybody always said yes, of course, and then went right on talking until you yourself considered it only a formality.

How long had it been since you had been listened to?

So you were quiet and did your driving and we got to the broadcast. I said that I thought some day there would be a library of scripts so that the actors would memorize their parts. I said I thought they were all paid too much money, that if there were not $18,000 at stake for an hour nobody would get so frantic that they would write a bad script just to have it fill up the time. I said if they were not paid so much money they would not get so confused and if they did not get so confused they would not mess up the works the way that Oakie and Erwin were doing that day.

And even though you had seen radio from its beginning you did not seem to think that they would have to keep on forever the same because that is the way they do it now.

You told me about Oakie when he first came to you and you said, He was very ingratiating, and I had never heard the word used in a pleasant sense before.

And when the broadcast was over you laughed and said, Here I so carefully brought my camera and I have not taken a single picture.

We went to your house and met your wife and the butler had got drunk and was gone and you were not going to have this make any difference, nor did you call the butler any names. And your old white dog was there everywhere, always under your feet like a footstool and at dinner he lay motionless under the table with your feet on him.

But before dinner you said some sentence which necessitated a fine distinction in its words. I do not remember for sure but I think you said A friend of mine, and then made yourself go back and change it to, acquaintance.

And I knew then that YOU HEARD YOUR OWN WORDS BACK.

And I got so excited I was covered with goose pimples. Am I to have it? I thought. Am I really to find it here, without any warning? Is it *now* communication?

For I had noticed with constant bewilderment that almost no one hears his own words back; so in order to understand what he says *you have to know beforehand* what he is going to say. Other people listen almost completely for the meaning and the tone of the voice because when they come in a room you can ask them to have a stove and they rarely notice but will sit down in a chair. They also then have decided what you are going to say before you say it and away from you will manufacture a quotation of what they thought you meant.

I was so excited at the prospect of being near this thing at last that I was very cold and kept my coat on all through dinner and the more you talked the more I knew that I was very close now, very close now and my hands were trembling so that I had to stop eating. I dared not try the cake, which was beautiful cake, and this hurt the cook, for which I was sorry, but you were very quick to help me. You said, I don't like cake either very much., and I was grateful to you.

Then at last it was over and we sat talking awhile before the fireplace and then we went out to your place. It had a lock on the door and no one ever came there but you and there was a little path of stones up to it. Inside was a huge fireplace before which sat two huge red chairs and opposite there a great desk where you sat. The inside of the window shades had designs on them—some kind of birds in bright colors. They did not seem like you. They have always puzzled me. And everywhere, on the floor, against the walls, everywhere were cameras and tripods and containers of developing fluid.

And we sat down and smoked and we began to talk. You *listened*, oh so carefully, the way I never knew anyone else to listen. You listened actively and with so many people it is a passive thing. And you never interrupted.

Once you were speaking of a movie and you forgot the title and you said, It is ridiculous not to be able to remember titles if that is your business. You gave yourself a little time and then it came out. And I saw how you would not let yourself get away with anything and fool yourself.

People are always saying, I never can remember names, or, I never can do this or that, or, Isn't that just like me? As though the things they could not do somehow gave them personality or character. Perhaps it does but it is not the method of a careful mind.

You said you had taken TURNIP'S BLOOD to Schulberg to read and he had said that he did not understand the dog's eating at the table. And you said to Schulberg, If you do not understand that I cannot explain it to you.

If you do not understand that, you said to me, you have never been lonely and that is all there is to it.

And yes, I looked at you and I admitted it. To no one else in the world have I ever admitted it. Not until that moment had I ever admitted it to myself.

We talked of Ruth Chatterton and of Julie Haydon and Margaret Sullavan (her voice) and you told me that I looked just like Maude Adams had when she was young.

You said that you always tried to read a manuscript in one sitting without mixing other things in between its parts and that is the way I had always tried to read books, with a *feeling of responsibility to the author.*

We talked all night and in the early morning we came in the house and you made coffee, not having to have anyone make it for you, and then your son came in and he and George took over and we were out, but it did not matter because I was perfectly contented to rest a long time and be quiet.

I had found a mind which did not fool itself, which would not let itself get by with any carelessness, which started over fresh without preconceived ideas on each new subject. I had found a man who knew the great importance of the meticulously chosen and carefully spoken word.

Most people do not have communication and they express this by saying they are not understood, putting all the responsibility on the listener, but the great responsibility is on the speaker, for when you get a listener you must be ready.

There was so much, so very much, and I can do no better job on you than I did on my sister.

But there were the things that showed through:

Your mind was disciplined.

You made yourself say what you meant even if you had to WAIT for it.

As you spoke a conclusion you revealed the mental processes by which you had arrived at it and, by your eyes, you showed that you were ticking off another's processes while he spoke.

If you expressed an opinion you said it was an opinion.

If you quoted you always gave the source and you always quoted the words exactly.

So many people do not like Bach and it is the same thing. They simply cannot listen to the notes one at a time. They try to listen for a phrase or for the way music makes them feel.

But all these wonderful things which I had never found before— they are leaving out your great tenderness for human beings and your very great humility before a man's potentialities, which is so different from the inverted self-conscious egotism called modesty, and your constant newness and your wonder at the world.

And there was another great thing. At the broadcast you had said it was really very doubtful whether a man had the right anyhow, to sell *Time*. And so I knew you knew about Time.

You took me to the station and you had everything perfectly timed and you kissed my hand and said nothing and left me. Outside you stood on the platform, not restless, not embarrassed, and we looked at each other for a minute exactly and then the train moved.

After so many years and so much trying, then I found it.

Communication.

For the first time in my life I was not talking to or at or over or under or near or far from.

I was talking *with* a human being.

And I knew that it was there and that it was real and I could tap it any time I wanted to.

When I had things I wished to say I would sit down, so easily, and write them to you. One day I saw some pigeons eating corn and I wanted to tell that and so I did.

Without interpretation.

Without explanation.

Without repetition.

This is what I traveled a thousand miles to tell you. *

People who have never sat in a room and talked intimately with Death (have a cigar, Death, let me get your slippers, Death), who have never called him by his first name, Time, who have never put on Death each morning along with the clean undershirt and buttoned him up securely, they do not know that all the false cheer is very fatiguing and that you do not want to be continually apologizing with your response for the state you are in. What you want is to know THAT YOU HAVE DONE SOMETHING.

And you, whose only real religion is service, I wanted to tell you that perhaps the greatest service you ever performed was not something that you *did*. It was by being what you *are*. For you gave me communication and in a place like the bare white salt flats, where there is so startlingly a black line for the telegraph and a black line for the telephone and a black line for the train and a black line for the road, you realize how ironic these things are. How bitterly you realize that people do not speak to one another.

So I came to tell you this and to THANK you, because you did it for me and I am a writer and perhaps I can do it for a great many others now.

Is it not what we are all of us trying to do?

But you said to write it and perhaps you knew that this would happen, that in writing this I would learn how to write. Perhaps that is why you said it. Even now I do not know.

Since that time I have seen how other people are beginning to

---

*this leaves out my concern for your health and the fact that I wanted to be with you if it were to be as bad as we feared.

be interested in this subject, communication. There is a book called THE HEART IS A LONELY HUNTER by Carson McCullers and there is a deaf mute in it. There is a book called JOHNNY GOT HIS GUN by Dalton Trumbo and the struggle of this eyeless, earless, legless, armless, faceless man to speak to a human being is the most dramatic thing I have ever read. It simply gets you by the throat and holds you until after years of tapping his head, he finally gets a LISTENER. But after that I think the book is false, because after such a struggle I do not think the thing a man had to say would be a lecture against war. I think it would be some very simple thing about himself. And then just recently I have been so thrilled to learn of a play on Broadway called JOHNNY BELINDA in which the heroine who is on the stage all the time never speaks until the last line. Think of sitting in that audience for two hours trying and trying to help that girl (also a deaf mute) speak. And with a lot of telephony and radio engineers the idea of communication is much more of an ideal than anybody thinks. And in CHU-CHU I tried this, too, to say that you cannot MAKE them hear by force.

But now I do not want to do this any more. I do not want to use any symbols. I want to say that with GOOD eyes and PERFECT ears and all their members, they still do not speak to one another. I want to say that it is not necessarily so. I want to say that communication exists.

And now there is another thing. I have always felt that you also had something to say to me. Perhaps some very simple thing about yourself. Perhaps something about writing. Perhaps your own mental autobiography. Perhaps it was the last telephone call.

When will I know?

I wanted to thank you for making it be the way that I thought it would be when I was very little. I would look at Mr. Whitlock and he would not have a veil over his eyes and he would not say anything silly. He would say I am Mr. Whitlock. There is a Whitlockness about me that keeps me from being Mr. Moore. No doubt you see it. And he would show me his whitlockness and I would show him my rachelness.

It docs not happen as often as I thought it would,

But it HAPPENS.

And what was the other thing now, that I wanted besides communication with people? I would look at a tree and it would shimmer all over—Well, it is different from the way I thought it would be, but

IT HAPPENS.

For the communication with things other than people I have to thank Mr. Fabre and I wish he were not so long dead. I wish I could thank him personally. For a landscape no longer looks like a picture postcard to me, static and finished and still. I no longer see a tree and over it the sky and under it the grass. Many many things are *going on* in that landscape and now I know it all the time. I look. Even looking from a distance I know it. For in the tree is a bird and on the bird is a louse and on the louse are bacteria. And from the branches of the tree hang beautiful complex spider webs and in the tree is a spider with her foot upon a sensitive telegraph wire attached to the web at the place of maximum communication. And in the grass and through it are wasps and beetles and flies and millions of forms all moving, moving, moving. And for each form there is one larger which preys upon it and one smaller which saps its strength as it also preys and saps, and the balance is constantly being adjusted. Even when the tree is dead it will not be still and stopped and suspended; for through it, eating a million tunnels, are the capricorn worms who, after three years, will eat to the outside and build a window and cover it up and lie down WITH THEIR HEADS TO THE DOOR and await the metamorphosis.

And so it does shimmer. It moves all the time.

So I thank you and I thank Fabre for making it be the way I thought it would be when I was very little and just seeking. I thank you both for giving me communication with all the things that live.

And why did it take you two, only you two, to make a DIFFERENCE in my life?

Many of the facts that Fabre tells I had read before and they did not stick, they did not become *mine*. It is because he NEVER omits the THINKING PROCESSES by which the facts are communicated. Even in the simplest little book on elementary chemistry written for his nephew and his son, even with the number of the elements all wrong and the terms outdated, the thinking processes are all there, just as good as they ever were, as they ever will be.

Many of the things you said I suppose I had heard before, but they did not register, but with you, when you speak, you speak with an awareness of the thinking processes and when you listen that is what you are listening for.

I wanted to tell you of the great and important thing you did for me and to show you the different places and the different ways that I had sought for it and had not found it. And telling it, I have learned a new way of writing—not a technique or a new premise or a new vocabulary, but a new DIRECTION.

I am not ready yet to turn upon CHU-CHU and say that it is no good. Perhaps for the people to whom CHU-CHU means something, it will mean as much as the new things I will write will mean to others, but there are fewer of those people. What is for the parlour is as good for the parlour as what is for the kitchen is for the kitchen. But there are more kitchens than parlours. Many many more.

By writing this to the only person in the world who could understand ALL of it *the way it is said*, I think I have learned how to write so that later things can be understood by any human being who has breathed the air in and breathed it out and learned to read and asked himself one question.

Thank you, dear wise and honest John.

September 17, 1941
Kansas City.

Notes to *Communication*

(Page 59, line 1): This is apparently a reference to a children's book that Rachel had read.

(Page 61, line 31): World War I.

(Page 65, line 8): A novel by John Steinbeck (1902–1968), published in 1937.

(Page 72, line 4): Jean Henri Fabre (1823–1915), whose book *Mason- Wasps* was published by Dodd, Mead in 1919.

(Page 74, line 14): "Mother of a Child" was published in the April 1938 issue of *Story* magazine.

(Page 99, lines 30–34): This statement is inexplicable in light of Rachel Maddux's often-demonstrated commitment to the celebration of human difference, and must have been made in response to a specific experience.

(Page 108, line 20): A 5 1/2 page description of the Theory of Fundamental Rhythm exists among Rachel's papers. The theory originated in her understanding of synaesthesia, and is derived from her study of physiology, psychology, and music.

(Page 112, line 23): Havelock Ellis (1859–1939) was the author of a number of books on human sexuality and also of *The Dance of Life* (1923; second edition 1926).

(Page 114, line 4): Cesar Auguste Franck (1822–1890) was an organist and composer whose major work was composed late in his life.

(Page 115, line 20): *R.F.D.*, a book about country life in Ohio, was written by Charles Allen Smart and published by W.W. Norton in 1938.

(Page 115, line 24): Havelock Ellis, *My Life*. Boston: Houghton Mifflin, 1939.

(Page 117, lines 33–34): Author's note.

(Page 138, line 29): Author's note.

(Page 141, lines 1–2): All of these were black jazz musicians. Mead Lux Lewis was one of Rachel's favorite jazz pianists.

(Page 143, lines 6–9): Rachel must have heard some of these stories much earlier, because in a poem titled "Girlhood," written when she was a child, she not only mentions a corn-cob doll, but footnotes this phrase to provide a description of the doll with corn silks for hair.

(Page 143, line 9): This story stayed with Rachel for a long time. In her March 30, 1983, column in the *Buffalo River Review*, she tells the story of her mother, at the age of eight, unwillingly having her ears pierced by her older sister.

(Page 146, line 1): George Corey and Savington Crampton

(Page 147, line 11): "We Are Each Other's Children" was published in the September-October 1938 issue of *Story* magazine.

(Page 147, lines 17–18): Georgie Stoll was the orchestra leader on the "Camel Caravan" radio program, and also music director for MGM. John Hammond was a wealthy man who encouraged black musicians; he was also a mentor to Benny Goodman. Milt Gross was a cartoonist.

(Page 148, title line): Last name deleted.

(Page 148, lines 30–32): Author's note.

(Page 149, line 15): Jack Oakie and Stuart Erwin, radio performers.

(Page 151, line 7): Budd Schulberg, novelist and screenwriter, began his career as a publicist for Paramount Studio in 1931. He is the author of *What Makes Sammy Run?* (1941), a satiric novel about Hollywood, and wrote the screenplay for *On the Waterfront* (1955).

(Page 151, lines 16–17): Julie Haydon first achieved prominence as the female lead in *Shadow and Substance* on Broadway in 1938. Ruth Chatterton (1893–1961) was a stage and screen actress as well as a film producer. Margaret Sullavan (1911–1960) was a film and television actress, who appeared in films in the 1930s and 1940s.

(Page 151, line 17): Maude Adams (1872–1953) was noted for her roles in Shakespearian plays. Toward the end of her career, she headed the theatre program at Stephens College in Columbia, Missouri.

(Page 153, lines 33–34): Author's note.

Turnip's Blood

Turnips do have blood, you know,
Thin and mauve and lighter than air.
And almost always so confined
One never sees it there.

Only when it spurts
As when a knife cuts through,
Or when the quantity becomes so great,
The turnip hurts

And lets it free, does one learn
That it was all the time
Made of multi-colored bubbles
That arise, expand and shine.

All his irritation at having been called out of bed at three o'clock in the morning was gone now. It had been a nice piece of work he thought, as he walked out of the hospital toward his car. He decided to drive the long way home and see the dawn because he wasn't sleepy and the weather was excellent, and he hadn't seen a dawn for years.

The long way around led through Miner's Village, a town of one street lined with two rows of identical stone houses. Lawrence had always liked Miner's Village and this morning he tried to think why. He felt quite sure that no one, not even the people who did live there, wanted to live there. Yet why was it so pleasing to him? The monotony of it must be the reason, he decided. Yes, surely the monotony . . . that was it. A lovely word in itself. He realized that he had gone through this reasoning before about liking Erik Satie's *Gnossienne*. Well, he thought, that was the difference between life and art—in art you liked monotony and in life you didn't.

If he knew more about art and less about life he might be able to write a treatise on that distinction which would forever shut up those stupid arguments about Is Art Nature? or Should Art Reflect Life? And then, Miner's Village miles behind, he thought if he had known more about art and less about life he might not have had the idea at all. He said, "Damn!" and knew he might as well be back at the hospital or asleep in bed for all the good he was getting out of being outdoors with the dawn coming up in a minute.

He stopped his car by the park when he got into town and got out to walk. It was a strange sensation to know that no one would be worried or conscious or even aware that he was wasting an hour. He felt a slight bit of guilt wash over him almost as though he had said he was glad that Edna was dead. It wasn't that Edna had not been a good wife; it was just that. . . .

He had missed the first moments of the dawn and that made him angry. He set his shoulders and determined to enjoy himself. And of course just when he had made up his mind to think of nothing but spring and dawning and being alive, there would be a whore sitting there on a park bench.

"My God!" he thought. "They're everywhere." The next moment he was terribly ashamed of himself because he saw that he'd been wrong and it was only a child—a very thin child sitting very still.

"Probably lost," he muttered to himself. David Lawrence had found, identified and returned to their mothers more lost children than any other one man in America. Lost children and beggars and women without tickets in railroad stations—he could spot them a mile off, and they knew it.

He sat down on the bench by the girl and realized that she was almost as tall as he and that she had an unlighted cigarette in her hand. So he had been right the first time! He had smiled reassuringly at her as he sat down and now he felt like a fool. What a ridiculous situation! Should he just get up and walk off? He was becoming more irritated every minute. She seemed to be unaware of his presence and went on just sitting there and staring in front of her looking fragile and contented and not like a whore.

"I beg your pardon," David said as he stood up, "I thought you were a child." Still she looked straight ahead.

"Yes, I know," she said.

"That's absurd," he growled. "How could you know what I was thinking?"

"But I am a child." And this time she did look at him.

"Well, why don't you go home then?"

"It isn't time yet."

"I suppose any time before six o'clock in the morning is too early to go home?"

"Exactly."

He could have walked away then, but he kept thinking she'd say something else. The air hung heavy with her silence and his anger and he wished she'd speak so that he could make a sarcastic retort. He wanted to make her angry. The seconds thudded by and he felt weaker and weaker and finally he sat back down again.

"What are you doing with that cigarette?" he asked.

"Holding it."

"Why don't you light it?"

"I don't have a match."

"Why don't you go get one? There's a store a half block away."

"It isn't worth it."

"If you have a match you smoke and if you don't have a match you don't smoke, is that it?"

"Is it so difficult to understand then?"

"And I suppose if you don't have any food you don't eat, and if you have food you eat?"

"Of course," she said. "It would be stupid not to eat if you had the food."

"Oh, God!" David said to himself. "It was such a lovely morning and I'm so mad. I'm so mad I could kill her."

"Look here. Don't you have a family?"

"Yes, but they aren't here."

"So they kicked you out?" he asked hopefully.

"No, I just left."

"Were they mean to you?" How could they have helped being mean, he asked himself.

"No, they were very good to me."

"Well, why did you leave then?"

"I was restless. They talked too much."

The city was thoroughly awake now and trucks and trolley cars filled their lungs with air and screeched for sheer joy. David Lawrence had a smile that he reserved for special occasions. He used it in the operating room when a clumsy nurse trod on his toe or when a piece of cat gut broke. The interns at St. Mary's knelt by their little white beds every night and prayed to Our Lady: "Please teach Doctor Lawrence to swear instead." He smiled so now and called over the noise of the traffic: "And you find it quiet and peaceful here?"

"Yes," she shouted, "I find it quiet here."

"Oh," he said, "you find it quiet here."

"And why is it," he asked, "that you can't go home until six o'clock?"

"It's because of Alice."

"Oh, I see . . . It's because of Alice. And *what* is Alice?"

"Alice is the girl who lives at night where I live in the daytime."

"And what does Alice do in the daytime?"

"She works."

"And you . . . you work at night—and sleep in the daytime?"

"Yes, that's right."

"If you don't mind my asking, are you working now?"

"No. I get off at four-thirty."

"Oh," he said, "you 'get off' at four-thirty."

Quickly she said: "Charlemagne immediately dispatched his herald, accepting the challenge, and said 'Bring me some soup.' There, repeat that!"

David Lawrence's spine snapped upright. "Charlemagne immediately dispatched his herald," he said, "accepting the challenge, and said 'Bring me a . . . bring me a . . .'"

"Bowl of soup," she said.

"Ah, yes . . . a bowl of soup."

"That's wrong."

"What's your name?"

"Eve."

Eve on a park bench, Lawrence mused, in a green sweater and skirt at ten minutes of six in the morning, still holding in her hand her four-thirty cigarette. He scratched a match and held it for her. She lighted her cigarette and looked up to thank him. Her eyes were green, too—very green, very narrow and very slanting. Her hair hung not very tidily down to her shoulders. It was vaguely curly and very thick.

"Your skin is very white, Eve," Lawrence said.

"Because it's never in the sun."

"What is this work you do until four-thirty in the morning?"

"I scrub floors in an office building."

He looked at once, of course, at her hands.

"That's a lie," he said.

"I wear gloves."

"So you saw me look at your hands?"

"No."

"Then—how?"

"It is the way one expects a surgeon to solve a problem."

"Then you know who I am?"

"I scrub the floors in your building. You're quite a legend there. The stenographer is in love with you."

"Which one?"

"The one with glasses."

"I think they both wear glasses," he said, suddenly aware that he had never recognized either of his stenographers as personalities.

"This one has gray eyes."

"I don't know what color their eyes are," he said, as though Eve was ridiculous to have thought he would have known.

"She has freckles—just a few."

"That's no good, either."

"She wears a pink dress, often."

"Pink dress," he said, "pink dress. No, I don't remember it."

"Her right shoulder is low and her left hip is high. She . . ."

"Oh, you mean Miss Simmons!"

"Yes," said Eve, "I suppose I do."

"Well, well. Miss Simmons. And what makes you think Miss Simmons is in love with me? I'm sure I never noticed it."

"She comes back nights to work and she has a newspaper picture of you on her desk which she puts in the middle drawer when she leaves."

"And *you* scrub floors!"

"Yes."

"Why? Is that all you can find to do?"

"I like it."

"You *like* it?"

"Yes, I like it."

"What's so charming about it?"

"Night work."

"So you don't like to work in the daytime?"

"Sun hurts my eyes and, besides, it's noisy."

So she's not a lost child, he thought, nor a whore; neither a salamander nor a shop girl.

Eve stood and yawned and stretched. "I have to go home now," she said, "it's after six."

"How can you tell?"

"By the noise."

"I have my car. May I drive you home?"

"No, I have to walk."

"Why?"

"It's on account of Rameses. He's afraid of cars."

"Well, may I walk, then, with you and—Rameses?"

"If you want." A sound came from Eve's throat—a hybrid sound half coyote and half bubbling brook. She turned her head toward David apologetically and said, "I can't whistle, you know."

"So I see," he said.

Infinitely nonchalant and dripping with sleep, Rameses padded slowly through the bushes, one ear alert, the other caressing his cheek.

"I see what you mean," David said. "It's hard to tell whether he's looking forward and going sideways or going forward in profile."

Rameses licked Eve's shoe. He put his elbows on the ground and let his shoulders melt into them. He sighed heavily and then stood up.

The three of them started off through the park, Rameses walking first in front, and then behind, then between the man and the girl. David stumbled a great many times.

"The dog gets underfoot just a little, don't you think?"

"He isn't used to walking with two people."

They walked four or five blocks from the park and then down an alley. They came to a fire escape and Eve said, "Are you hungry?"

"Starved."

"What time do you have to go to work?"

"Nine o'clock."

"You'd better eat then. Come on." They climbed two or three miles into the sky and Rameses and Lawrence had a hard time of it because Rameses was far from agile and Lawrence was dizzy. When they got to the top Eve pushed open the door and said, "Don't bump your head."

The floor was bare and clean. There was an odor of damp wood and laundry soap unpleasantly mingled. The walls and ceiling looked like a freshman art student's idea of cubism. In fact, they looked like anybody's idea of cubism. Against one wall there was an unpainted wooden table with two straight chairs; along the adjoining wall, a wooden bed with neither head nor foot, slightly too wide for a coffin. The third wall had shelves holding books on one side, dishes on the other, and a door leading into the bathroom. The other wall was cut into by a window and the door they had just entered. The room looked restrained rather than poverty stricken; severe rather than bare.

"Sit down," Eve said, and disappeared into the bathroom. Lawrence heard her splashing about and presently she reappeared very shiny and barefooted in a clean but shapeless gray garment which came to her ankles.

She raised the window and reached outside into a box fastened to the ledge, bringing back cheese and milk, two fresh pears, unsalted butter and a loaf of pumpernickel. She set these down in a chair while she spread a coarse but very clean cloth over the table. Then she stacked everything in the middle of the table, and set on opposite sides of it two squat red glasses, two blue plates and two blue cups. She put a knife by each plate and a bread knife by the loaf of bread. She disappeared into the bathroom again and came back with a pot of coffee.

She went once more to the window box and brought out a package of meat which she put on a newspaper for Rameses.

"All right," she said to Lawrence. The whole process had not taken more than fifteen minutes, and yet in that fifteen minutes Lawrence had learned more about the power and the courage of color than he had dreamed of in his fifty years.

When Lawrence had been thirty he looked and acted forty and now that he was fifty he still looked forty. It seemed to him that he had always been forty and not feeling fifty, he did not allow himself to say those things that people of fifty can say quite naturally without being thought too sentimentally sincere. So he did not tell Eve that the red glass seemed to be the source of light for the room, but he said instead, "I never knew a table could look so pleasant," hoping she might think he referred to the food and to his appetite.

"It's because the walls are white and the room is bare and my dress is gray. Then, too," she added, "pottery is so much warmer than china."

"Young girls," he thought, "can say things like that and it sounds all right." They ate and did not talk much except for a slight discussion on coffee and its noble qualities.

"Do you call this breakfast?" David asked. "I've always been curious about people who turn day and night around."

"I eat only once a day," Eve said, "like Rameses, so it doesn't matter what I call it." When they finished Eve lit a cigarette and pushed her chair back against the wall. She asked David if he liked to smoke a pipe.

"I smoke a pipe at home," he said, "but I never carry it with me." She went to the bookcase and brought him a pipe and a can of tobacco.

"You can smoke this one if you want," she said.

David chuckled. "Alice's?" he asked.

"No, its mine. I always run out of cigarettes at the end of the month."

She sat down and tilted her chair against the wall and finished her cigarette. Then she got up and put the remainder of the food back in the window box, took the dishes to the bathroom, set them in the tub, and turned on the water. While it was running she took the cloth from the table, put her chair in place, transferred Rameses's newspaper from the floor to the waste basket and returned to the bathroom. She turned off the water in the tub and as she dried each dish she set it on the shelf, except for the coffee pot which she left on top of the stove in the bathroom.

She spread two blankets down on the floor and opened the window. She put a blanket on the table by Lawrence. "It gets cold sometimes," she said. She went into the bathroom and washed her teeth. Coming back into the room, she set the alarm clock for eight.

"I have to go to bed now," she said. "Don't let Rameses out when you go." She sat down on one edge of the blanket and covered her feet securely. Then she lay down and, catching the upper corners of the two blankets in her teeth, her arms at her sides, she rolled over and over until she had exhausted the blankets. Rameses, from his corner oozed over to her side and lay down. Slowly he lifted one ox-like paw in the air, reached and touched her like a priest giving his blessing. He closed his eyes, sighed, and slowly his leg relaxed and slipped to the floor.

David laughed at the sight until Eve's head popped turtle-like out of the bundle of blankets.

"Why don't you sleep on the bed?" he asked.

"It's Alice's," she said and withdrew her head.

Lawrence sat and smoked Eve's pipe and listened to the breathing. Eve had gone to sleep at once and her breathing was even and rapid and quiet. Rameses snored erratically and now and then a leg twitched and the toenails scratched back and forth on the bare floor.

"Dreaming of rabbits, no doubt," Lawrence said to himself as he knocked out the pipe and laid it back on the shelf on his way out.

Chapter Two

Lawrence was a man of considerable mental discipline. As he said, "he had to be," and so he neither neglected his work nor lost his sleep over Eve. But he was cursed (or blessed) with an accurate and vivid memory. The same thing that made him able to remember every patient's name and idiosyncrasies made him see Eve in her long gray robe when he smoked his after dinner pipe at home.

The next day a patient, a young girl, came into his office wearing a green sweater. He found himself being less brusque, less professional in his manner with her. The day after, he asked Mrs. Darling, his cook, to get him some pears for dinner and as he ate them he pronounced Eve "plain stupid," but he got up at five-thirty the next morning all the same and drove to the alley and parked by the fire escape to wait for Eve. He would have liked to go to the park again, but he didn't feel up to another tango with Rameses.

Presently Eve turned the corner about a hundred feet from him and came into sight. Rameses trailed behind. She pushed her hat onto the back of her head and began hop-scotch jumping, landing with one foot on each block of sidewalk. Each time a foot came down she paused for a moment stork-wise and said, "He will come," or "He won't come." She ended face to face with Lawrence just as she said, "He won't come." She was out of breath and looked surprised to see him.

"So much for superstition," she said, and started up the steps, her hat still on the back of her head. David stood bewildered on the sidewalk.

"Aren't you going to invite me to come up?" he asked. She stopped climbing and, leaning over the hand rail, looked down at him.

"Oh," she said, "didn't you come to see me?"

"Of course I came to see you."

"Then why are you standing there, then?" she called.

As he started the long climb the doctor muttered to himself, "For this I get out of bed at five-thirty in the morning."

As he bent his head to go through the door he saw the flowers on the table. He went over and stood in front of them for a moment before he took off his topcoat.

"How many years it's been," he said, "since I have seen a larkspur!"

"I hoped you'd come before they died," she said. He knew then that they had been bought for him and he was pleased and felt shy. He turned to look at her, but she had already gone into the bathroom and closed the door. Presently he heard her splashing and singing in a cheerfully loud, but not very good, voice.

Everything was the same as it had been before except that there were apples instead of pears, and after Rameses had been fed and the dishes washed, Eve didn't go to bed but sat on with her chair tilted back against the wall.

He had thought of a lot of questions he wanted to ask her, but it didn't seem to be quite the right time.

Suddenly Eve jumped up and, taking him by the wrist, pulled him into the bathroom.

"Shh!" she said

"What's the matter?" he whispered.

"The collector for the gas company is coming up the stairs," she whispered back.

"I don't hear anything," David said, forgetting to whisper.

Eve frowned at him for answer and after a few seconds David, too, could hear the steps. While he stood there he realized that the bathroom was the one place that could not be seen from the window.

"Must have done this before," he thought. He wanted very much to laugh.

Eve said "s-s-s" through her teeth, and Rameses went to the door. In answer to the series of knocks that followed, Rameses sent back terrible sounds. They were frightening enough, but not exactly what one expects of a dog. David visualized his looking back over his shoulder and saying sweetly: "I can't bark, you know."

The collector left and Rameses gave one look around for approval and went to his corner.

"Is it safe to go out now?" David whispered, enjoying the secrecy of a shared danger.

"It's all right now," Eve said.

"Can I go after him and pay him, Eve?" David asked.

"Don't bother," she said. "It's only a week till I get paid, and besides the coffee's gone too, so it just came out even."

"You mean they turn the gas off?"

"Sure."

"How'd you know who that was, by the way?"

"Recognized the footsteps. He has metal plates on his shoes. Didn't you notice?"

"You should have been a detective," he said.

"Or an Indian." She smiled and walked over to Rameses to reward him for his bravery with a pat on the head which he acknowledged with a yawn.

"Shouldn't you go to bed?" Lawrence asked.

She didn't answer for a few seconds and then she said, "You'll come back again?"

"Yes," he said. Then he remembered the flowers and added, "If I may."

"Then I'll go to bed."

He felt that he should have gone then but he couldn't resist watching the blanket rolling ritual, so he sat down and had another pipe. He looked at the flowers and smiled and then he looked around the room more conscious of detail than on the previous visit. There were a dozen or so worn books on the shelf and he put on his glasses and went over to look at them.

Conrad Aiken's *Jig of Forslin* was there and *Easy Recipes for Newlyweds* and a sagging, shabby dictionary. *Sanine* and Huneker's *Painted Veils* stood erect with difficulty to support Anderson's *Winesburg, Ohio* and *Care and Feeding of the Dog,* which were aslant. *Daphnis and Chloe,* thin and shy, stood between a history of alchemy and *Gargantua and Pantagruel.* Carlyle and a Norse mythology approved each other over their beards of ravelings, while *The Circus of Doctor Lao* stood aloof, blatant and conspicuous in its newness.

"They could be Alice's," Lawrence told himself as he tiptoed out.

He got in his car and drove down to the gas company. He wondered if she'd be angry at his paying her gas bill. He knew he was a person that many people feared and he had always rather enjoyed helping his temper out a bit and so he was amused at finding himself a good fairy.

"I'll have to get a wand," he thought. He stopped the car and strode into the office, unconsciously adjusting himself to the civilization of "business."

"I'd like to pay a bill," he said to the man-at-the-desk.

The man-at-the-desk said, "Do you have the bill with you?"

"No, I don't," David said.

"What is the name?"

"Eve," said David. He blushed and looked around in panic. He didn't know her last name. Why hadn't he thought of that? Nor did he know the street or the apartment number. It was impossible to say to the man: "You go down Chestnut Street, see, and then you turn left down an alley."

"I beg your pardon," he said. "I have forgotten the name." He almost ran out of the building and pushed the revolving door so hard that he had to go around twice before he could get out.

He climbed into the car and swore as he saw the man-at-the-desk running toward him.

"You left your billfold, sir," he said.

Lawrence took Eve for a ride the next morning after Rameses had been fed and left in the room. They stopped to eat at a restaurant and Lawrence started to order his usual breakfast, but thought in time to order cheese and bread and fruit and coffee. He was surprised and rather pleased to find himself capable of such subtle and flattering tact, but Eve spoiled it all by asking him what he usually ate for breakfast.

David was not after all so different from those very people who were in awe of him that he could resist the telling of something that had embarrassed him, and so he told Eve about the episode at the office of the gas company wondering, as he told it, whether she would be angry at him for having tried to pay her bill or properly chagrined at not having told him her name.

If it has been said that the doctor had a smile, then it should certainly be said that Eve had a laugh. It came straight from the belly without suppression or apology. It was robust; it was sustained; it was loud. The tears streamed from her eyes and after she had found her handkerchief and blown her nose, she said, "Did the man ask if you were Adam?"

Lawrence was at first shocked that she showed no sympathy for his embarrassment, but he soon came to see the picture in Eve's mind of Adam, dressed in his fig leaf, holding his billfold (for which he had no pocket) and saying to a twentieth century man-at-the-desk: "I have come to pay Eve's gas bill." It was the first time Lawrence had laughed with Eve and he found it pleasant.

When they had finished breakfast, David asked: "Eve, what do you want to do?"

"Oh, I'll have to go home," she said.

"I don't mean that," he said. "I mean what do you want to be? Aren't you ambitious? Do you want to go to school, or what *do* you want to do?"

"I went to school."

"How long?"

"Through college."

"You mean you got a degree?"

"Oh, no, I didn't get a degree."

"How long did you go to college?"

"Four years."

"What was the matter—did you fail?"

"Oh, no."

"Well, why didn't you get a degree then?"

"Well, you see, you have to be present at Commencement."

"Of course, weren't you?"

"I couldn't bear the thought of it," she said.

"But didn't you think you'd need it when you went to get a job?"

She laughed at this as she had laughed at the picture of Adam and Eve and said: "Oh, can't you just see Mrs. Glutcher and Mrs. Peabody and me all standing in a row holding our mops in one hand and our sheepskins in the other?"

He realized as he became irritated with her that he must have been thinking more about her than he would have liked to admit. He saw that he had made of her a child with an impossible dream and of himself a benefactor.

"Then you're not ambitious," he stated rather than asked.

"No," she laughed, "I don't care what I do when I'm grown up."

He knew that he had said a thousand times that ambition ruined women, that he would love, just once, to find a woman who wasn't ambitious, and now that he had found her he was provoked. He had occasion almost weekly to comment unfavorably upon what he called the modern generation, yet when Eve refused to fit his idea of that very generation he was angry with her for it.

"Did you learn anything in college?" he asked

"Oh, yes," she said. "I learned to hate football and vocations and efficiency and routine."

"Didn't you learn to love anything?"

"You don't *learn* to love things," she said in dismay at having to explain such a simple fact to him, "they happen to you."

He was no longer irritated at her, only amused now and relieved that he had solved the mystery. "The purely emotional type," he tagged her mentally and smiled to think of the various complex solutions that had crossed his mind vaguely since he had known her.

He took her home, his mind quite at rest, and as he left her, knowing he would not come back, he was aware of being disappointed that she no longer interested him.

It occurred to him on his way to the office that he still did not know her name. Then he realized that if he ever wanted it he could ask the building manager.

Chapter Three

The doctor, certainly, was not a "purely emotional type." His mind was of the reasoning texture which makes of a geometrical theorem a pleasure, of the elimination of irrelevant details a habit, and the deduction of a logical conclusion a necessity. So it was inevitable that the little details about Eve, inconsistent with his classification of her, came to insert themselves into his consciousness until they got on his nerves.

"What I ought to do," he said, "is to have a look at her academic record just to satisfy myself." So, supposing she had gone to the state university, he wrote for a copy of her transcript (with the building manager's help) saying that he wished to give her employment. He realized that he was not being very much of an adult about the thing and that he might just as well have asked her himself.

He got a polite letter in answer reminding him that he had forgotten to enclose the customary fee. He swore and reached into his pocket to find that as usual he had no money with him. He wrote a check and mailed it, wondering after he had sealed the envelope if he had remembered to sign it.

By the time the transcript came he had ceased to think about it and for that reason the record amazed him all the more. She seemed to have excelled in all possible fields with the exceptions of domestic science, pedagogy and sociology which she had not studied. She had, Lawrence saw by a more careful scrutiny of the record, failed consistently in physical education, hygiene and economics. She had once failed in metallurgy, but had repeated the course with a high mark.

Had he asked for a letter of recommendation he might have learned a great many other interesting things about Eve, but he never felt it necessary to take another's estimate of a character when he had a chance to form his own.

"Can the universities really be so bad," he asked himself, "or is it that I was so wrong?"

But finding Eve not academically stupid did not change his attitude.

"If she's not stupid," he growled to himself, "she's arrogant . . . and that's worse." But he had to admit that he had always cherished his own arrogance.

"Well, at any rate," he decided, trying to settle the matter, "I wasn't in love with her and that saved me from being ridiculous." The fact that he had stayed sane and impersonal and unimpressed seemed to please him and then:

"Or did it?" he asked himself. He thought of blackmail, he thought of finding an hysterical charwoman in his office. He saw the facts divorced from their situations: a man fifty, relatively well to do, a girl nineteen or twenty scrubbing floors, unable to pay her own gas bill.

"It's all too possible," he said, "I'd better put a stop to this before it happens." He put on his hat and strode out of his office and realized that Eve would be asleep at this time of day. He decided to wait until the next morning, but by that time he had come to see that Eve could not be put into facts, that no expression of years would describe her naiveté, nor would facts express her charm.

He was angry at himself for being so suspicious, so unimaginative and he was glad that he had not gone to her in anger about something which he felt she would not have been able to comprehend.

He might never have gone to see her at all but for a book he read one night in which there was a minor character, a child of fourteen of whom it was written:

"She had always an air about her of a recent scrubbing and a robust appetite which made her hands singularly incongruous. They were so delicate, and the bony structure was so little concealed, that they looked brittle."

He never finished the book nor learned what became of the child with the "brittle hands," for a procession of Eve's hands as he had seen them in a hundred different dynamic attitudes passed before his eyes and obscured the print. He laid the book aside and counted up the hours before six o'clock in the morning when he should touch Eve's hands for the first time.

As he fell asleep that night he did not wonder if her hands would be brittle or soft or firm or cold or warm. He thought only that they were somehow pathetic.

He got there at six o'clock and, when she didn't come, he thought she might have come home early or his watch might be slow, so he went up alone. There was no answer to his knock and it occurred to him that she might have gone away. He wished frantically that he had not waited so long to come back. He tried the door and found it unlocked. He had not really expected it to open and he ducked his head and stepped in feeling very guilty. The books on the shelves were still there and he found her gray robe hanging in the bathroom.

He grew impatient waiting for her and so aware of the silence that he wished for some kind of activity. It occurred to him that he might have a meal ready when she came, but he could not find the first thing he wanted. He marvelled at the ease with which Eve had made the little meal appear and at his own inability to make the first definite move. He stood in the middle of the room looking vaguely about him as though to find a tablecloth and silverware hanging from the ceiling.

So Eve found him when she came. She stood speechless just inside the door and automatically kicked it shut behind her. Then, as though she had followed the thoughts that had brought him back to her, she came toward him with her arms outstretched and put her hands in his. She grasped his hands so tightly that she hurt him and then as quickly she let him go and stepped back.

He wished to confess, to apologize. She could have made it easy for him. She could have asked him where he had been; why he had not come. Because she didn't he could not make the effort and so he said: "I wanted to have breakfast ready when you came, but I couldn't find anything. Where do you hide everything?"

She laughed at him and said: "I bury it." Then she went into the bathroom and took up her usual morning routine as though he had been there only yesterday.

When they had finished the meal he asked, "No larkspur to-day?"

"It turned red," she said, "and I had to throw it away for insubordination." She was thinking as she said it of all the lark-spur that had bloomed and died in that room since he had last been there, of how, having had such luck the first time, she had become superstitious about it and had thought at each new vaseful that he would come before it died.

"You look tired," she said.

"I am," he answered. "I almost lost a woman yesterday. That takes it out of you, all right. Yes, it takes it out of you."

"Do you care each time," she asked, "as though it were the first time?"

"Yes," he said, "I guess you do. You tell less people about it; that's all."

"I'd heard you couldn't—that you didn't dare."

"You heard wrong," he said, and then, as though the subject were uncomfortable for him, he put his elbows on the table and leaned forward.

"Eve," he said, "I've been wanting to get you a present, or do something for you, but I don't know what you want. You don't want to go to school; you're not ambitious; you seem so satisfied, and I'm so bad at buying presents. Eve, don't you want *anything?*"

He wished he hadn't said it at all. He thought he should have left her just as she was. He had always felt that people did harm who gave children half dollars when they still believed coppers worked magic. He wished he had drunk his coffee and left things as they were. He felt clumsy and heavy and he lifted his eyes to hers and saw there the light of conquest, the rapture of Aladdin.

"Do you mean I can have anything—that you'd do *anything?*"

"Well, I'm not Midas, you know. I have my limits." He laughed doubtfully.

Eve, too, had put her elbows on the table and leaned very close to him.

"I'm so excited," she said. "I'll tell you what it is I want more than anything. I want Rameses to sit up at the table on a chair and eat with me . . . with nice manners. I've tried and tried and I can't teach him."

David felt as Charon would have felt had a passenger offered him a handsome price to row him to hell. Had she asked for jewels he would have been disappointed, had she asked for a merry-go-round or a ferris wheel he would have been amused. But to be asked to turn animal trainer to an aged and sad-eyed hound of doubtful if startling ancestry, that was surprising. It took him some little while to relax and arrive this far in his conclusions but suddenly he saw the really surprising angle of the whole thing, beside which the request was a mere extending of the palm.

"What makes you think," he asked, "that *I* can teach him if you can't?"

"But of course you can," she said. She did not say it to bolster up his courage as mothers say to their children: "Of course you can go to school by yourself." She stated it simply and like "hot is not cold; cold is not hot."

Something like this unquestioning faith he had seen a few times in his patients taking their first unhampered steps. Some of them could not keep their eyes on his face as he told them. They could not resist looking at the floor, but a few walked toward him without once looking down. Even these were not like Eve because they tried so hard. Eve did not try to have faith in him, he saw. She could not even help it; it came so easily.

"You must think . . ." he began.

"Oh, never mind," she said. "If you don't want to. I only thought—you said . . ."

"Of course I'll try," he said quickly. "I just don't know if I can, that's all, and then I was so surprised at the request."

"Why?" she asked.

He balked at the futility of trying to explain to her, and turning to Rameses said: "Well, when shall we begin?" Rameses, unsuspecting what trials lay ahead of him, slept peacefully in the corner.

Eve went over and woke him. She pushed him toward David gently and said: "Do you be a good pupil, now!"

"I'll not watch," she said to David. "I want to be surprised."

While Eve slept, David tried in turn his bedside manner, his club manner, his manner for the children of friends, all equally without avail. He took off his coat. He lifted Rameses onto the chair saying "sit up, sit up," and patted him on the head. Then he lifted him onto the floor and said, "sit up, sit up." Rameses's feet grew roots into the floor.

David put on his coat and washed his hands and left in disgust. He stamped down the fire escape, muttering to himself: "I'll be god damned if I'll be an animal trainer. I'll tell her. I'll tell her that dog of hers is too stupid to learn anything. I'm surprised he can even eat off the floor. It's a wonder she doesn't have to feed him with a spoon! Maybe she should get some seals, too. She could keep them in the bathtub and I could throw them fish. Fish!" He stopped one floor from the ground and ignored his dizziness in the excitement of his discovery.

"Of course," he thought "You have to feed them to teach them tricks. Any food would have known that."

He was back the next morning with a sirloin steak cut into neat cubes. Rameses, of course, didn't know the difference between sirloin and boiling beef, but David didn't know that Rameses didn't know it.

By the time that the sirloin was consumed, Rameses had progressed so far as to be able to clamber up one leg at a time from the floor to the chair. He did it with no grace whatever after the manner of a fat, rheumatic and aged Negress boarding a bus. But grace was of small concern to Lawrence; he could find that elsewhere. He was seeking accomplishment, pure and simple.

Lawrence learned, as he was urging Rameses to progress from the four-legged to the two-legged method of sitting upon chairs, that dogs as well as people have that benign and complacent acceptance of over-indulgence which makes them take after dinner naps without pangs of conscience. For all he had once scorned the chair, Rameses now went to sleep on it, although it was incapable of supporting both his body *and* his head. He seemed to smile as he slopped over the edges of the chair as though to say: "It's silly of me, I know, but I just can't help it."

After that, Lawrence got half the amount of steak and cut it into twice the amount of cubes.

Rameses had learned to climb from the floor to the chair at command in two days. In a week he ventured so far as to sit upon three legs, lifting the fourth in the air, but sit upon two legs he would not. They were set back by the fact that Lawrence, by calling Rameses all kinds of flattering names in a gentle voice and holding the meat cube tantalizingly close, had persuaded Rameses to take both front legs off the chair for a second, whereupon Rameses fell onto the floor upsetting the chair. It was two days before he would even approach the chair again.

Lawrence petted Rameses. He fed him, cajoled him, talked to him, and finally he swore at him in German, French and Spanish.

By the time they again reached the three-legged stage, Lawrence had come to remarking to himself that by this time he could have bought Eve the crown jewels of Czechoslovakia, built her a mansion with his own hands, or raised a St. Bernard from a pup and taught him to eat with chopsticks.

Every morning for two weeks Eve asked with bright expectancy: "Can he do it yet?" to which Lawrence, from long experience, answered: "He's coming along," or "Pretty soon, now." It was difficult when she asked each morning, but when she ceased to ask and nobly, if obviously, avoided the question, David's heart sank.

He pleaded the necessity of a trip to a medical meeting in a distant town and stayed away for three days. He had planned to stay home and read in books whose pages held no word of dogs, but he found it much easier to work, or to give up to thinking more about Rameses.

"I don't know which keeps me at it the more," he said to himself, "whether I hate to let Eve down, or whether I'm too proud to admit failure."

The next morning at eight he went to Eve's apartment and asked if he might borrow Rameses for the evening and bring him back the next morning. He was a little hurt at her slight show of reluctance, but he made no comment and with one hand on Rameses's collar and the other on the steering wheel he drove to his office. Remembering Eve had said Rameses was afraid of cars, he spoke reassuringly to him all the way down to the office. Rameses shrank and trembled, but Lawrence was flattered (and at first disgusted and later amused at finding himself so) by the fact that Rameses in his fear huddled near him.

Lawrence unlocked the door of his office and found Miss Simmons hard at work. He wished that Rameses had been a mouse which he could have hidden in his pocket, a bird in his hat, a cockroach in his hand.

"I just came back to do a little work," David said. "Brought the dog along for company."

"Can I help?" pleaded Miss Simmons ardently.

"Oh, no, Miss Simmons, thank you. But it's nothing you could do. Besides, you shouldn't be working such late hours. Is the work too heavy? Should I get someone to help you? You mustn't let us impose on your good nature here, you know. Better take it easy."

"Oh, Doctor Lawrence," Miss Simmons blushed, "you don't give me *half* enough to do. I always like to come back at night and do the little extra things."

"That's very kind of you, Miss Simmons, but you must go now. You've worked enough for one day. *Somebody* has to watch out for your health. If you won't I'll have to."

The chance to be protected was too much for Miss Simmons. She put on her coat and left. She giggled all the way home and said, "Let *me* do that, Miss Simmons. . . . You shouldn't work so hard . . . ."

In the safety of her own room she allowed herself to weep. "Oh, my Darling," she said to the wall, "you're so kind."

David locked the door upon Miss Simmon's back and sighed with relief.

"Rameses," he said, "you'll make a fool of me yet." Rameses was lifted onto a table and told that he was a good dog. He was patted on the head and strapped into place. He was exposed to the emanations of the X-ray. He was then released, measured and taken in the horrible car to Lawrence's house. Here he was fed and shut in the basement for, while Lawrence had always liked dogs, he didn't believe in being sentimental about them. As Lawrence prepared to climb into bed he heard Rameses howling in defiance at his solitude.

"He'll get used to it," Lawrence said, as he pulled up the bed clothes. "A little discipline won't hurt him."

He soon learned that he could either go to sleep or else he could "discipline" Rameses, but not both, so he got out of bed and swore as he tried to get his arm into the wrong-side-out sleeve of his bathrobe. When he opened the basement door Rameses lunged at him and, unmindful of the fact that he had almost knocked Lawrence over, he wagged his tail in gratitude and made that series of sounds which passed with him for barks.

He followed Lawrence upstairs and into his room and there he made a careful olfactory search for Eve and familiarity. Finding neither, he walked the floor.

"If only you could put your hands behind your back," Lawrence said, "then it would be perfect."

They exhausted themselves finally and when Lawrence awoke it was to find Rameses by his side, his cheek upon the pillow.

David returned Rameses to Eve and at her exuberant welcome of the dog he wondered whether it were a simple greeting or relief from anxiety.

"What have you two been doing?" Eve asked.

"That's a secret," Lawrence said.

He went to his office and studied the X-Ray picture of Rameses's spine. As a roller-coaster for thrill craving couples of meningococci, or as a slow motion picture of the falling of the Tower of Pisa it would have been excellent, but placed upright it would hardly have supported a new born fly.

Laughing to himself and shaking his head from side to side, the doctor designed a brace for Rameses. It was an intricate affair with laces and buckles and chamois-covered pads. He sent the specifications to the man who made his braces and along in the afternoon he got a puzzled and apologetic telephone call from that meticulous person.

The brace-maker had made mistakes in his time and upon his head had fallen the doctor's red and purple wrath. So he asked if he had read the directions correctly, if there had possibly been some mistake?

Lawrence repeated the dimensions from memory, assured the man curtly that all was well and closed the conversation.

Now this maker of braces believed with all his heart that if the doctor were to tell him something should be seventeen thousandths of an inch and he were to make it eighteen thousandths, Lawrence would undoubtedly detect the difference. He fussed about his work so much at home that his wife often wished he would take another job, but the brace-maker always said to her: "He worries the life out of me, all right, but I like him, all the same. You see?" His wife did not see and the brace-maker finally gave up trying to explain it to her.

He looked at Rameses's brace when it was finished and said, "Maybe a snake stubbed his toe; maybe a hunk of baloney has gone limp. I give it up."

He sent the brace to Lawrence still fearing he had made some mistake, but he heard nothing further from it.

The next morning Eve said, "What's in the package?"

"It's a secret," Lawrence said. "You're not to see it yet. It might not work."

It did work, though, and in a few days Rameses, wearing his pale pink brace, was able to sit up on his haunches and eat off a plate on the table. The time had come to show Eve and Lawrence made her sit at the table with her eyes closed until he had got the dog trussed up.

"All right," he said. "You can open your eyes."

"Oh!" Eve said. "Does it hurt him?"

Somehow, Lawrence had expected gratitude. "Oh, no," he said. "As a matter of fact, it probably feels good. At any rate, the feat is impossible without it."

Eve held her breath and waited.

"Sit up!" David said to Rameses, and Rameses jumped upon the chair, sat up and ate, his corset strings dangling behind him.

Eve jumped up and hugged Rameses. She clapped her hands. She squealed. She danced about the room and finally she sat on Lawrence's lap and put her arms around his neck.

"I'm so happy!" she screamed. "You're wonderful."

Lawrence said: "You specified 'nice manners,' but you'll have to do that yourself. I gave up at this point. Besides, that's a mother's job anyhow."

Suddenly pensive, Eve said: "I just thought of something; now we'll have to get another chair."

"Oh, no," David said, "just put mine on a newspaper on the floor."

"I wouldn't think of it," she said quite seriously.

Chapter Four

They planned to go on a tour of second-hand furniture stores the next day to find a third chair like the other two, but when Lawrence parked his car in the alley Eve came flying down the fire escape at a pace that made him shiver.

"We're not going shopping," she called. "Come on up. I've had news."

David waited until he had safely climbed the steps before he spoke.

"You're home early, aren't you?" he asked.

"I've quit."

"Quit?"

"Just last night. I've a new job. Did you ever want anything for years and years and then have it come true? I'm so excited. But wait, I'll show you the letter."

She was hopping up and down in her incoherent excitement and she picked up the letter from the table and waved it in front of him so that he could not have read it even if he had had his glasses on.

"Child, child!" he said, "stop jumping. Calm down now and tell me what it's all about." He put on his glasses.

"It's a circus," she said. "Isn't it wonderful?"

"You're a circus, certainly." He took the letter from her. It really was a circus. He read the letter through and then said, "You're not serious?"

"Of course I'm serious."

"You mean you're going to join this circus? You're actually going to travel about in a dirty little old train with a bunch of freaks eating rotten food and ruining your health?"

"It isn't like that at all, I'm sure. Of course I'm going. I've wanted to all my life and I've been trying to get this job for three years. Isn't it wonderful? Aren't you excited?"

"No, I'm not," he said taking off his glasses. "It's perfectly absurd. My dear, you've got a lot of crazy ideas in your head and I'm going to get them out. Now, see here. . ."

"Oh, you don't understand," Eve said, all her excitement apparently gone, "and I thought you would."

"I understand this. You're a child who needs a good spanking. You've got a lot of pretty ideas in your head. You're not a delayed adolescent; you haven't even reached adolescence yet. Why . . . Besides, what could you do in a circus? Have you even thought of that, now?"

"I'm going to ride a white horse, so there!"

"I suppose you told them you wouldn't come unless you could ride a white horse?"

"I said a white horse or an elephant."

"An elephant would have been safer at that. Have you ever been on a horse?"

"Once; that's how I knew I'd like it."

"Oh, I see," he said, "once."

Before they had eaten, he simply spluttered his anger at her, but after the meal he had calmed down somewhat and tried to reason with her, to explain to her the sordidness of the life she was going to. He might as well have tried to convince her that the Lorelei wore a wig or that the odor of Christmas trees was dimestore perfume. He saw that it was quite hopeless and that he was only making her impatient and unhappy, so he accepted the fact and wished her luck.

"When do you leave?" he asked.

"Tonight."

"So soon? I suppose you will be so great and famous that you'll scorn the society of a mere doctor when you come back?"

"I'll write to you every day and tell you all about it," she said. "Besides, it's only for a few months, you know. I only want to see what it's like and get to know the people."

"Don't tell me you're going to write a book about it?"

"A book?" she asked. "What for?"

"You just plain don't have any excuse at all for going, do you?" he asked.

"I don't need any."

He stood at the door wishing either to try again to dissuade her or to tell her how much he would miss her, but he had not quite forgotten his anger and could not bring himself to say anything.

"Well, goodbye." he said.

She put her arms around him and kissed him. Not having expected any such show of affection, he was very awkwardly holding his hat in front of him and Eve held him so tightly that he could neither get his arms free to put them around her, nor could he save his hat from being crushed.

"If I miss you too much," she said, "I shall come back right off."

Miss Simmons came into Lawrence's private office three days later holding an opened letter in her hand. She blushed and stammered as she held it out to him.

"I'm so sorry, Doctor, but the letter was not marked 'personal' and I just supposed it to be office business. I'm awfully sorry I opened it. I do hope you'll forgive me . . . ."

Almost every day one of these letters came and, until Miss Simmons had learned the handwriting, Lawrence was continually being embarrassed. Eve, in her naiveté, never thought to mark any of the letters "personal" and, since she travelled perpetually and never mentioned in advance where she was going, he could not write and tell her to address her letters any differently.

Elkhart, Kans.

May 15th

Dear David:

Rameses and I live in a big car which is just like a house inside while the circus goes from town to town. The man on the flying trapeze's wife and the Fat Lady live here, too. They did not much like having Rameses at first, but when I had him show them the trick you taught him, they were won over. The Fat Lady laughed and laughed and asked me to ask you if you would make her a corset. She is not allowed to wear a corset when the show is on, but she says she wears it while she's resting because it's more comfortable, except the stays in this one punch. She offered to show me where the stays punched, but I declined. The Fat Lady is very jolly. She told me all about her husbands. The first one was a sailor and the other two didn't seem to be much of anything. She did not mention where they are now, but I gathered that she considers herself well rid of them.

I would have written to you last night, but I was hypnotized by watching the man on the trapeze's wife do her exercises. She insisted that I feel her calf muscles of which she is very proud, and she offered to show me some exercises to get me over the horse-stiffness. I tried a few, but finally decided the horse was the lesser evil.

You were right about the food, but the coffee is good.

Love,

Eve.

P.S. The horse's name is Solomon and he really *is* white.

Hugoton, Kans.

May 16

David:

So far I've just sat on Solomon, but today I began standing on him, first on two feet and then on one. It feels just like it looks, only they won't let me laugh while I do it—only smile.

I wish you were the Tall Man or something, so you could be here, too.

The Bearded Lady came to call on me after the show, and what do you think? She's really George Bernard Shaw in disguise! She gave me the position (financial, social, marital, unmarital) of the members, a concise little paragraph for each, and offered to advise me on my choice of friends. She smoked up all my cigarettes so that I had to borrow off the Tall Man who is fast becoming my best friend. You know without my telling you, of course, that he likes Rameses very much, and vice versa.

'Till Sublette,

Eve.

P.S. Who does your charring now?

"As though I'd know," David said to himself. He laughed over the letter and, as was his habit, he mechanically tore it up and threw the pieces in the waste basket. Immediately, he wished he hadn't. The later ones he saved, carrying them home with him at night to the desk in his library.

Sublette

May 17

Dear David:

Whomever this town was Sublette to got a raw deal. The dust is knee deep. Even Solomon looks gray.

On account of Rameses, I thought it wise to make friends with the cook who is a big Negro named Sam. Today the Tall Man told me Sam said he wanted to see me and when I went over, what do you think he had bought for me? An orange and a head of lettuce. I didn't dare eat it in front of anybody he said, because they'd get sore if they caught him playing favorites, so I stood back of the kitchen and chewed it down like a rabbit. Sam said he used to cook in a big hotel in Tulsa and he could tell a lady when he saw one and knew what they liked to eat. I didn't say a word.

It seems a long time since I saw you.

Eve.

Garden City

May 18th

Mon Ami:

Today I got to ride on an elephant. There are two and I had such a time deciding which one to choose. It is lots of fun, like a slow motion of rocking in a rocking chair, but not nearly as much fun as riding on Solomon. I'm glad I do not ride the elephant in the show.

The man who rides the elephant in the parades and shows is the only person around called "mister." He is Mr. Carmichael, and he is most impressive looking, like King George. He joined the circus (that is, Mr. Carmichael—not King George) when he was drunk and signed a two year contract, but he takes it most philosophically.

I asked him what he used to do, but he said that it had been so long ago that he couldn't remember.

He promised to take me to visit the snake charmer who is quite exclusive and hard-to-know.

Eve.

P.S. Rameses sends you his love.

Dodge City
May 19

Dear David:

Mr. Carmichael and I found the snake charmer smoking a cigar and reading an old movie magazine. She likes Mr. Carmichael because they're both Irish, that is, she's half Irish and half Indian and that is a combination you shouldn't miss. Even without the paint, she's a scream.

Mr. Carmichael told me she didn't have time to be nice to most people because she had to paint those pictures on her every day. He was only kidding me because she's really tattooed.

She asked me where I came from and when I told her she said: "Have they got any real artists up there that can do tattooing?"

I told her I wasn't acquainted with any and she said to Carmichael: "I been thinking I'd like to have some more work done by a really high class guy. I'm getting tired of what I got and I got lots more space, but every place I go they only got the same old patterns."

Rameses is getting so fat you wouldn't know him.

Love,
Eve.

Kinsley, Kans.
May 20

Mon Cher:

Do you know this country? It is perfectly flat as far as one looks and all day I have hardly seen a tree. Yet the whole thing beats and beats as though all the people who had walked across this land in coarse and clumsy shoes had left the rhythm of their tread. The sunsets escape being melodramatic by getting over with quickly, like a farm woman in labor who is used to having babies. It is the first time I ever really felt "America."

Solomon has at last recognized Rameses and the three of us are now good friends. I shall hate to leave Solomon.

I still get hungry at six o'clock in the morning out of habit. Do you?

Yours,

Eve.

Larned

May 21

Dear David:

We had a poker game last night and I won all the Clown's money. I offered to give it back to him, but he would not take it. His name is Arthur and he is much funnier with his own nose and eyebrows.

He has got the political situation all analyzed and he explained it to me. At the time it seemed quite clear, but right now I cannot seem to remember much about it except that if the politicians would do as he says he would no longer be a clown in a circus that only boasts two elephants. Instead, he would be back in vaudeville juggling at eighty a week. As I say, he explained all this very carefully to me, and after he had aired his opinions of circuses like ours (already I'm possessive, you see) I felt that he and you would have a great deal in common.

Authur tried to initiate me into the fine art of juggling, but whether it's apples or dumbbells they all come down on my head. I do not have the slightest talent, but contrary to my expectations, this did not make Arthur angry or impatient with me. I had proved beyond a doubt that, just as he had said, juggling is a very difficult art and scarcely appreciated by the uninitiated.

Arthur says there is a revolution coming, so you must get ready for it. You may even wish to leave the country, because if I understand Arthur correctly, one will find, after the revolution, millions of highly paid jugglers and jugglers only on every theater stage in America.

The man on the flying trapeze and his wife have patched up their quarrel (for the good of the act, they say) and he has quit travelling with the cotton candy man and the ticket taker to come back to us. When the Fat Lady heard the news she said to me: "Now it won't be dull around here any longer, dearie. We'll have some roarin' good fights."

If it gets too bad I shall go live with the lion in his cage, for he is so old that his teeth are all soft and he is so fond of his keeper that it is only with the greatest difficulty they make him roar any more at all. It is for this that I call him Robert Ingersoll. Even that does not make him mad.

Love,

Eve.

Great Bend, Kans.

May 22

David:

We got paid today. It hardly seems right to get paid for having so much fun. When the Fat Lady found out how much I made (or rather, how little) she had a fit of rage and said my youth was being taken advantage of. But really I can hardly do any tricks yet and I ride sitting most of the time, so I think the Fat Lady is being quite unreasonable.

Everybody here has got kodak pictures of somebody in their dressing rooms. I wish I had one of you.

Love,

Eve.

Lyons,

May 23

Dear David:

I have been trying for several days now to learn to ride standing with one foot on each of two horses. You've no idea how difficult it is, and the only other white horse in the show is not so nice as Solomon. I am supposed to have it perfect for the McPherson show, but I don't know if I shall be able to or not.

Authur wants to use Rameses in his act but I am not sure if I could bear to have him laughed at or not, and yet it is hard to refuse Arthur anything. It means so much to him whether one hundred or two hundred people applaud.

If I do not lose all my money at poker, I shall buy a victrola when I come back.

Love,

Eve

For several days David did not hear from Eve and so he read her old letters over. They so amused him that he wished there were someone he could show them to. He had few intimate friends and even with these he feared being thought ridiculous, so he laughed alone. When the next letter came he opened it before he had even examined the rest of his mail. The lines slanted across the page, characteristic of letters written in bed, and David was stiffly apprehensive before he had read the first word.

> MERCY HOSPITAL
> McPherson, Kansas
>
> Dear David:
>   Would you pay for having Rameses sent to you and take care of him? No one in the show could take him because they had to go on. I got stepped on by a horse, I think, and I'm in the hospital here and they won't let Rameses come in. He has stood at the door for three days now.
>   Please wire, because he must be awfully hungry and I can't get them to let him in.
>   I don't know when I shall see you again, but at least the circus days are over.
>
> Eve

"The crazy little fool!" David said. "She *would* get herself hurt. And she hasn't even sense enough to write what is the matter with her, but fills the whole letter with anguish about a dog. What does she think a hospital is?"

He was so angry that he did not come to be concerned for several minutes. A long distance telephone call got him in touch with her physician and thus it was that he learned of the terrible and tragic accident that Eve had described as having been "stepped on by a horse."

He told Miss Simmons to postpone all his appointments and he prepared to leave on the next train.

Waiting in the railroad station with characteristic impatience, he suddenly remembered Eve's one request. She had neither asked him to call the hospital nor to come to her and both of these he was doing; but she had asked him to take care of Rameses, and he had done nothing about that. He called Miss Simmons and asked her to locate a veterinarian in McPherson and to wire him sufficient money to care for Rameses who could be found at the Mercy Hospital door.

Then he boarded his train. He had brought nothing with him to read and he raged with impatience at every stop. He tried to sleep and found it impossible. The rhythm of the train kept reminding him of one of Eve's songs.

Have you never heard of Gertie the Goon?
She's half a ghoul and half a loon.
She isn't dead yet, but she will be soon.

He counted up the time he would be away from his office and tentatively arranged his schedule on his return.

Oh, she lives all alone in a great big house
Built from the skin of a great big mouse.
She sits in her parlour and she bays at the moon:
"God! don't you know that I'm Gertie the Goon?"

Damn that song! Surely Miss Simmons would telegraph if anything went wrong with that boy in 214. How many days had he been in?

She had whiskey for breakfast and brandy at noon,
She chewed up licorice and ate with a spoon.
Her skin was yellow and her eyes were blank
And once a year she bathed in an old tin tank.

He tried to think of another tune to drive this one from his mind. The woman in the seat in front of him was chattering in a shrill voice. David rose and went into the smoking car.

She got high on the weed and low on rum
She fastened her kimona with chewing gum.
And she did up her hair with safety pins.
Oh, Gertie the Goon knew all of the sins.

Where did she learn such songs? Children these days! He remembered some of his own student days. After all, he too had once sung songs. Well, yes, of course. . . . But, then. . . . He chuckled at some vaguely remembered episode and, feeling his laughter incongruous, remembered Eve's accident. How would she take it? He must be careful not to say "I told you so."

Once in McPherson, he went straight to the hospital and sought out Eve's physician. He found it somehow awkward to explain his presence there in an unprofessional capacity and muttered something about having been a friend of the family's.

"I'm very glad you have come," the doctor said to David, "because she has consistently refused to tell us how to locate her family. I don't think yet that the full force of her condition has made its impression, although I have explained to her plainly that she can never walk again. She shows absolutely no despair, and at the same time her attitude does not seem to be one of forced courage. Really, a most curious case—and yet, a most amiable patient."

"May I see her, now?" David asked.

Eve was much paler than usual, and there were gray splotches under her eyes, but otherwise there seemed no change in her. She did not seem either very surprised or very glad to see him and for greeting asked: "Did you take care of Rameses?"

"Of course I did," David said, "but it's you I came to see. How are you?"

"I'm tired," she said. Never to walk again, without money and undoubtedly in pain, she chose of all things to say that she "was tired."

"Well, I must say," David said, "you seem to take the whole thing lightly." She seemed to be so little in need of sympathy that he was at a loss for words. In all his years of practice he had never seen a patient so unconcerned as Eve, except those who wished to die.

"You do not know," Eve said, "how comforting it is to know that no one will ever again expect ambition of me."

Was this, David asked himself, that enlightenment that America needed to understand her youth? Were these children who believed that knowledge was for pleasure and endeavor an empty thing—were these the progeny of pioneers? Was youth, then, not mad, not radical, but only tired? Or was Eve an exception, a sprite in a real world? No, he thought to himself, there is no great generalization to be learned here; there is only a child to be taken care of.

"I shall have to live on the ground floor when I come back, won't I?" Eve asked. "And, not go up to the attic."

"Dear Eve," David said, "you shall have to go back to your family."

"Oh, no," Eve said, "they'd make me work cross-word puzzles, trying to keep me busy, and they'd be everlastingly sorry."

"But you can't live alone," David said.

"Then I shall come and live with you," said Eve.

"Unfortunately, you're hardly of an adopting age."

"Then you shall have to marry me," she said.

It was two months of gradual transition before David, too, came to this conclusion and in the end the two conclusions were identical and David's voicing of it did not sound as much weightier than hers as it should have in the view of the fact that it took his sixty times as long as hers to be born.

In the manner in which they decided to marry they were like two people shopping for hats. David must go to all the stores and see all the hats in order that, after he had bought the first, (which he had really liked) he need never in the future have occasion to doubt the wisdom of his purchase. Eve was as one who buys a hat to cover a head. This, of course, is only for analogy, for were they really shopping for hats, the doctor would have gone to the store where he had always bought his hats and where the clerks knew so well what he wanted that they would give him the right one the first time. And what Eve would actually do in a hat shop is unpredictable.

The doctor "looked for his hats," so to speak, from all angles. From thinking the situation impossible, he came to thinking that Eve was not old enough to choose a husband. She should marry a young man. Then he remembered that Eve, paralyzed, would hardly be in a position to choose.

He did not, of course, think of the matter constantly. Sometimes for days at a time the whole idea seemed so unreal and his work so real, that he scarcely gave it a thought. Then he would find himself saying things like: "I could fix over the library for her. There is a fireplace in there and it's downstairs. I could take my stuff upstairs."

He half heard some music on the radio one evening that brought Vienna back to him. There it was, crystallized before his eyes, full blown and in its glory. Eve had never seen Vienna. What fun it would be to tell Eve about Vienna—Vienna of twenty-five years ago, before anyone guessed that She was dying. He thought of Eve's sitting across the table from him (the table was so large; perhaps it would be nicer to sit around one corner) and of his telling her about Vienna and of walking in Switzerland, and of how he could tell her just enough and from such an angle as to give her a good appetite.

There were so many things that he had seen and read and learned. He could not help but realize how pleasant it would be to have a curious and eager child in the house to tell them to.

But the thing that finally decided him was a startling realization of what he would be able to do for Eve. It was remembering her remark about the cross-word puzzles that set him to thinking of this aspect, for he saw without conceit that of all the people Eve should probably ever meet he was best suited to the job of taking care of her. He would neither watch her with apprehension nor obviously ignore her limitations. He would know that there were times when she need not be "occupied" at all, and when time did hang heavy on her hands, how ingenious and varied the diversions he already knew and how many more he would think of under the impetus of necessity.

He gave himself at least twenty more years. In twenty years she would be forty something. What would become of her if she stayed with her family? If they were still alive at that time she would have had behind her twenty barren years of attention, solicitude and cross-word puzzles. And if he took care of her for twenty years? She would at least have money enough for servants and she would have a house to be interested in in a way that it is impossible to be interested in another's house. And, if he at all deserved his success or his reputation, she would not have an invalid's mind.

"When you look at it that way," he said to himself, "it seems cruel and stupid *not* to marry her."

It did not really matter that it had taken him two months to come to the decision, for Eve could not have left the hospital before that time anyhow and under no circumstances whatever could David have brought himself to feel that a hospital was a suitable place to be married in.

He made the trip to McPherson to get her when she was released from the hospital.

"I thought," he said, "that we could be married here and then go straight to my house because the drive will tire you, I expect."

"All right."

When he had got her lifted into his car and had assured himself that she was as comfortable as possible, he suddenly remembered something and asked: "But where are your things?"

"I sent them to your house yesterday," she said.

He rather expected her to follow this remark with another or with a smile which would accentuate her cleverness at having known that he would, after all, marry her, but she looked ahead at the long flat highway, apparently having forgotten the remark.

Once she turned her head to look directly at him and her smile was such a one as to make him feel warm and glad and she said: "How good it is to see people in real clothes again!"

Chapter Five

David felt that he had been right about the library, for the room pleased Eve. She had been there a week, in fact, before she showed even any curiosity to see the rest of the house. David was not sure that Eve could see the rest of the house comfortably, for she had firmly refused to have a wheel chair brought into the house, saying that they, like pianos, never seemed to belong in a room. David himself carried her into dinner each evening and, since he saw her only in the evenings and she never complained of any inconveniences during the day, he thought that in this first week she probably was still weary enough to rest most of the time and that Mrs. Darling was so far succeeding in making her comfortable.

So when Eve said she wanted to be shown the rest of the house by him he suggested that perhaps it would be better to wait until they had time to figure out the best way (meaning until Eve had reconciled herself to some kind of conveyance) he was surprised to hear her say, "Oh, Anthony will carry me."

Anthony was a huge white-haired Negro who had come to work for David so long ago that the circumstances had been forgotten. At any rate, he had come before Mrs. Darling, who had once been the cook and was now housekeeper. For what specific duties David had hired him originally neither of them could remember. He had been retained because of his philosophy, which was neither very clear nor very constant, but always colorful.

Anthony, whom David had always thought old and lazy, Anthony knew just how to do it. Eve, like a dancer in mid-air, dwarfed to feather size by contrast with Anthony's bulk, looked at David over Anthony's shoulder as he followed them up the stairs.

"You see," her eyes looking mischievously at him said, "a wheel chair is a clumsy and an ugly thing and for me it is unnecessary." David was much amused, as he always was at the sight of male servitude to a female whim. He was always amused at any human trait supposed to be characteristically "masculine" or "feminine."

Eve asked a great many questions in all the rooms and then she said she was tired and wanted to be taken downstairs.

They had slipped into a routine which they found pleasant. They met first for the day at the evening meal. They lingered long over coffee and cigarettes, and if David did not have to go out, he would take Eve on his lap and they would talk about what they had done all day while they had been apart. Then he would settle down to do the writing or reading or thinking he had marked out for himself that day.

Eve usually sat across the room from him while he worked and, when she got tired with reading or sitting, he carried her into bed and helped her to undress. While she yawned loudly he read her a bed-time story from a book for children. While he read she held his free hand in both hers. At first he had been alarmed at the amazing number of bed-time stories he should have to hunt out, but he soon found that one would last for weeks, for Eve went to sleep so quickly when she was tired, and she was so seldom able to remember the next night where she had left off listening, that as a result David read the first pages over many times.

Although he read them to her to put her to sleep, he was sometimes so defeated by the slow progress they made that he was tempted to awaken her and plead with her to hold her eyes open until they could get past some particular paragraph which was beginning to bore him.

One night, though, he finished one complete fairy tale and Eve was still awake. He was so astonished that he asked her if she were ill or restless.

"No," she said, "curious."

"Not about the story, surely?"

"Take off your clothes," she said.

The Mermaid and the Fisherman fell to the floor and David was suddenly thankful that he had kept up his golf and swimming.

"You look like a horse trader, the way you're staring," he laughed at her as he undressed.

"Oh, I'm so glad," she said.

"Glad?"

"I was so afraid you might be wooly," she said. "It's so nice to know you're all smooth." She smiled and fell asleep.

He stood for several minutes estimating the possible chances of meeting Mrs. Darling if he should walk upstairs without dressing. He hated to dress, only to undress again as soon as he had reached his own room. He decided to chance it and, holding his clothes over one arm, he leapt silently up the stairs and into his own bed.

"I'll bet," he mused "that Eve would have liked to have had that in the marriage lines: 'I, Eve, take thee, David, if thou are smooth and not wooly.'"

David never failed to be surprised and amused at Eve's conversations when they talked together in the evenings. He always gave her a brief outline of what he had done during the day and usually he asked her how she spent her day. Almost always she had some long tale of purely imaginary and highly amusing activity to relate to him, and strangely enough, there was no tone of irony or bitterness in the telling.

Eve usually had flowers in the house and one evening David noticed a huge bowl filled with chicory flowers. They were held together by a piece of florist's paper lace.

They both had been looking at the chicory when David asked. "Well, what did you do all day?"

"I've turned alchemist," she said.

"So?"

"Uh-huh."

"Are you a member of the union?"

"In excellent standing."

"Are you making gold?"

"No, my activities are purely experimental. Today, for instance,

I threw Stravinsky and Huysman and Caldwell into a cauldron. Then I stirred and stirred, all the time humming the Star Spangled Banner to make it boil faster. And what do you think I got?"

"A burn?" David hazarded.

"No, a pink elephant. A small pink elephant. Next, I put in W. H. Hudson and the elephant's ears were edged with lace. When I added Van Vechten and a little aqua regia the elephant's front legs disappeared and after Cummings had finally dissolved the hind legs, the poor thing rocked back and forth on its belly most pitifully."

"You didn't leave it like that?" David asked.

"Dear, no. I said to it: 'Poor thing, how will you move?' Without any other change of expression, the legless elephant simply lifted one eyebrow and said, 'There is no longer any place I wish to go.'"

"How strange," David said, "that pink should be the mark of sophistication among elephants."

"I thought," Eve continued, "that the way things were going, the kindest thing I could do would be to make it disappear altogether, and so I reached for my copy of Jean Cocteau to that end, but by some mistake I threw in Carlyle which was next to Cocteau on the book shelf (God knows why!) and the whole thing turned into a bunch of chicory flowers wrapped in paper lace!"

"You don't say," David said.

"And there they are for evidence," Eve said, "right in front of you."

And so they were.

Chapter Six

As he mounted the stairs this evening, he wondered what adventure she would have made up for today. It occurred to him that she might not have any at all. He was frightfully late for dinner. Eve had never seemed to be aware of whether or not he came home early or late, but he knew from long years of experience what a state Mrs. Darling would be in, and he did not expect Eve to remain uninfluenced by Mrs. Darling. Though she had bullied and nagged at him for years, David had never thought of asking her to leave. Mrs. Darling was plump and Irish and she "spoke out frank," as she said, but David did not believe that any other cook would be different. He had never really taken her managing and grumbling very seriously. Certainly, he never sent patients away from his office because of what Mrs. Darling might say about his being late to dinner. But, on the other hand, he did not sit down after the last patient was gone and smoke his pipe either. He came home.

Edna had agreed with Mrs. Darling that a late dinner is a spoiled one, and Edna had often repeated Mrs. Darling's scoldings in Mrs. Darling's words, but with her own pronunciation. It had often irritated him, but since he considered his tardiness unavoidable, he could ignore the comments.

Eve was still in her own room reading and so David did not find her in the dining room. He thought she might have been angry and not waited for him.

"Has Mrs. Lawrence already eaten?" David asked of Mrs. Darling.

"She has *not*," said Mrs. Darling, "though what there'll be for her to eat *now*, I don't know."

"I expect she's in her room, then," David said, eager to escape.

"Probably fainted away with hunger, you'll find her," said Mrs. Darling.

But Eve was reading a book, sitting a chair before the fireplace, Rameses at her feet, and she put up her face to be kissed as though a dinner might be eaten without discussion at any hour.

"I'm sorry I'm so late for dinner," David said, "but . . ."

"Oh, is it time for dinner?" Eve asked.

"Mrs. Darling is in a state," David said.

"So, that's what she was muttering about!"

They giggled quietly like two children who have hidden their nurse's shoes. David was as happy as he had been the day they hid in the bathroom from the bill collector. Mrs. Darling stomped into the library and found them giggling.

"You'll not find your dinner so funny," she said.

"Oh, is it ready?" Eve asked.

"Is it ready?" shouted Mrs. Darling. "Is it *ready*! It's *been* ready since six o'clock."

David carried Eve into the dining room and when Mrs. Darling had left them, she winked at him. David was thinking that it was all too good to last and was about to say "Two against the cook" when Mrs. Darling reappeared.

She set a steak before David and, looking slightly over his head, said: "You'll find it cold."

"That's all right, Mrs. Darling," he said.

"There's some as don't mind *what* they eat," she said. She did not leave the room although there was no further need of her staying. It was obvious that she expected, almost anticipated, further argument. David found himself enjoying the situation. With Edna he would have felt belligerent, but Eve's presence had changed the situation to one of amusement. He was startled to see unmistakable anger on her face. He felt somehow disappointed, as though he had expected too much of her.

Eve was not eating. She held her napkin clenched in her hand and her eyes were narrowed.

"Mrs. Darling!" she said, "are you a Catholic?"

In all the years that Mrs. Darling had stood near a table, no one had ever asked her such an irrelevant question, nor had anyone dared to speak to her in such a voice.

"The Lord be praised, I am, Ma'am," she said, turning to Eve.

"Would you *dare*, Mrs. Darling, would you *dare* to tell the priest you thought the Virgin Mary was an Irish slut?"

Inside Mrs. Darling was created suddenly a vacuum—a vacuum that audibly sucked air into her mouth.

"The saints forgive me should I dare," she gasped. Eve seemed to be growing taller.

"In this house, Mrs. Darling, my husband is God, and nagging at him is blasphemy. This is *his* house and if he doesn't get home until midnight, it's all right, do you understand? It's quite all right. He's supposed to have his meals when he wants them, and it's your business and mine to see that they're hot. If he didn't work so hard that he *had* to come home late, neither of us would even be here."

Nothing had ever so surprised David. He could not remember that anyone had ever defended him. He felt pleasantly important and suddenly he knew that he loved Eve terribly. The sight of Mrs. Darling, however, changed his noble reverie into sheer amusement. Mrs. Darling, perhaps for the first time in her life, was chastened. There is nothing that so throws cold water on Irish indignation as finding spirit where it is unexpected. Mrs. Darling was silent. She was silent all over. Her bristles visibly wilted. David had a fleeting wish to be a fly and to dart into her open mouth. Very quietly she said: "Yes, Mrs. Lawrence," and padded softly out of the room.

Eve turned to him, her face a picture of tender consideration. "Are you ill?" she asked him.

"No," he said. "Why?"

"Fights always made my father sick," she said.

"On the contrary, I'm convulsed," he said. Mrs. Darling safely out of hearing, David felt free to laugh. He laughed at Right Defended and at the memory of Mrs. Darling's open mouth and he laughed because he felt good.

"What are you laughing at?" Eve asked. She could have understood his being angry—even his being sick—but not his being amused.

He could hardly stop laughing long enough to ask, "What would you have done if she had been a Methodist?"

"Why, I . . ." Eve hesitated. "I should have thrown a plate at her."

Lawrence never again was scolded by Mrs. Darling for being late to meals, but he was never able to convince Eve that the incident had been funny.

Apparently without compunction Eve had left him to join a

circus. She had greeted him at the hospital without surprise and she had sat through the marriage ceremony as though it had been a parent-teachers meeting. So it was natural that as the days wore on David thought that he might have interpreted her defense of him to Mrs. Darling as a manifestation of love only because it had so shocked him.

Except for Mrs. Darling's attitude, their days were unchanged. The diversions that David had planned were never necessary. He marvelled that Eve seemed never cross or restless. Almost every evening's conversation showed him new colors and textures in her mind. He found himself suddenly smiling at odd moments during the day at the memory of something she had said. He was as surprised at her knowledge of the stage directions for operas as he was to hear her singing:

She was a harlot and I was a thief,
And we loved each other beyond belief.*

but his knowledge of her emotions rested unsteadily on her delight in Rameses's trick, her fight with Mrs. Darling and her otherwise constant equanimity. His work during the day and his evenings with Eve served to make both so enjoyable that he found himself accepting the life pleasantly and easily without question, except that now and then he was puzzled about either the absence or the obscurity of her emotional depth. Had it not been for the scene with Mrs. Darling, he would not have been puzzled. Had she really married him, then, because of his remark that she was too old to adopt? But then, what of the larkspur? Had it not been bought for him? What of the hat-crushing caress? Were woolliness or smoothness essentials of pseudo-adoptions, of friendships? "Why question?" he asked himself. "She seems contented; I am quite happy. What does it matter?"

One evening after dinner he found his cigarette case empty. They searched the downstairs fruitlessly, and Eve said, "I left my cigarettes upstairs in the attic. Would you get them for me?"

---

*My Uncle Oswald by Roy L. McCardell.

On his way upstairs David remembered that weeks ago Eve had asked him if she might redecorate a storeroom upstairs. He had said that of course she might, thinking that it would give her something to do, and, since she had not mentioned it, he had forgotten it until now. He was curious to see her ideas of decoration and he wondered if he had given her enough money.

He turned on the light and found himself back in the old attic where they had first been together.

This room was larger than the old one, but not unlike it in shape. There were the same table set for two people with the same bright colored dishes, the same two chairs, the books and the pipe on the shelves. Even Alice's bed was there. He sat down in one of the chairs and tilted it against the wall and allowed himself the luxury of memory that is not sad because it is not over. He got up and walked about the room and delighted in checking over every detail. Everything was there except the fire escape.

And then he saw something was different. There was a niche that had been made in the wall and resting in this was a study of hands which had been carved from wood. If he did not find the study beautiful, he found it fascinating. The hands were not passive, but the fingers had been caught in movement and he was aware of knowing kinetically what the movement was going to be. And then of course he knew. They were his hands. The wood was of mellow brownness; the surface dull from oil. The veins and hinted wrinkles were accurate testimony of his own labor. The sudden and surprising tapering of the fingers—the moonless nails—all his. Even his ring was there; the ring he wore on his little finger. It, too, was a little large. It, too, seemed to slip to one side.

He left the light burning and ran down the stairs. To Eve, whom he had left in the dining room, he said: "Those hands . . . they're mine."

"Yes," she said, "they're yours."

"Who made them?"

"I did."

"But how?"

"From sketches," she said, "hundreds of sketches in the evenings while you were working."

"The whole room . . . it's . . ."

"You forgot the cigarettes," she said.

"So I did."

He carried her into the living room and went back after the cigarettes which were on Alice's bed. That night he did no work, for he had to hear every detail of the room and of how she had carved the hands and how often and patiently Anthony had carried her up and down stairs, and of the difficulty of buying Alice's bed. They talked very late, and Eve went to sleep on his lap. He carried her into her room aware that he held something infinitely precious and amazing.

All the next day he kept thinking that surely she loved him. Finding the room, and, most of all, his own hands there like some kind of idol in a temple, made him not afraid to voice what he had feared to read into the larkspur or the subduing of the Irish.

So, when Anthony called his office and said he thought he'd better come home, he said he'd come at once, without even asking what was wrong with Eve.

He found Anthony, Mrs. Darling and Eve all in the attic.

"What's wrong?" he asked. Anthony stood silent, the picture of helplessness, his head bowed in the presence of something too much for him. But Mrs. Darling was not silent. Mrs. Darling was frankly exasperated.

"She's been going on like that for hours," she said, "Just cries and cries. She says she's not sick, but she won't stop cryin'."

David sent them both away. He found himself more irritated than relieved that the fall or illness he had imagined was really hysterics. He said all the things that he would have said had Eve been a patient. He was firm, brusque, kind, calm, patient and firm again. All this filled a pillow slip and both his handkerchiefs with tears. He resolved to wait and "let her cry it out." She seemed capable of going on forever. Finally, he did what the most stupid of his patients would have done under the circumstances. He took Eve on his lap and put her red and swollen face against his shoulder. He kissed her and patted her head and while she blew her nose an endless number of times he told her over and over that he loved her.

When she was quiet and almost dry he asked, "What was it, Eve dear?"

"I don't know for sure," she said, sniffing, "but I think . . ."

"Yes, dear, you think . . . ?"

"I think I'm growing up," she said.

A Bibliography of the Published Works of Rachel Maddux

Novels:

The Green Kingdom. Simon and Schuster, 1957.
Abel's Daughter. Harper and Brothers, 1960.
A Walk in the Spring Rain. Doubleday, 1966.

Nonfiction:

The Orchard Children. Harper and Row, 1977.

Short Stories and Novellas:

"Turnip's Blood." *Story Magazine*, December 1936. (Reprinted in *The Flying Yorkshireman*, Harper and Brothers, 1938.)
"Mother of a Child." *Story Magazine*, April 1938.
"We Are Each Other's Children." *Story Magazine*, September-October 1938.
"The House in the Woods." *Collier's*, February 3, 1945.
"Final Clearance." *Fantasy and Science Fiction*, February 1956. (Reprinted in *The Best From Fantasy and Science Fiction*, Sixth Series, Doubleday, 1957.)
"Overture and Beginners." *Fantasy and Science Fiction*, September 1957.
"The Clay Pigeon." *Star Weekly* (Toronto, Canada), October 24, 1959.

Communication, the Autobiography
of Rachel Maddux, and Her Novella,
Turnip's Blood was designed by Dariel Mayer,
composed at The University of Tennessee Press
on the Apple Macintosh, and printed and bound
by Braun-Brumfield, Inc. The book is set in
Trump Mediaeval with Galliard display and
printed on 60-lb Glatfelter Natural, B-16.